ENGLISH SKILLS
BY OBJECTIVES

BOOK ONE

ENGLISH SKILLS BY OBJECTIVES

BOOK ONE

Grammar Fundamentals

This book is derived from

an instructional program

created by the

AMERICAN PREPARATORY INSTITUTE

Central Texas College, Killeen

CAMBRIDGE Adult Education
Regents/Prentice Hall
Englewood Cliffs, NJ 07632

Cambridge gratefully acknowledges the advice and contributions of the following adult educators who reviewed the draft version of this book:

Donna Amstutz, Chicago Urban Skills Institute, Chicago, Illinois.

Janet Moore, Coordinator, A.B.E. Section, Birmingham City Schools, Birmingham, Alabama.

Denise Schultheis, Springfield Community Schools, Springfield, Ohio.

Nancy Sullivan, Jersey City Learning Center, Jersey City, New Jersey.

Project Editor: James Fina
Production Manager: Arthur Michalez
Managing Editor: Eileen Guerrin

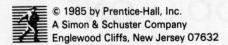 © 1985 by Prentice-Hall, Inc.
A Simon & Schuster Company
Englewood Cliffs, New Jersey 07632

Printed in the United States of America

10 9 8 7 6 5 4 3

ISBN 0-8428-0213-4

Prentice-Hall International (UK) Limited, *London*
Prentice-Hall of Australia Pty. Limited, *Sydney*
Prentice-Hall Canada Inc., *Toronto*
Prentice-Hall Hispanoamericana, S.A., *Mexico*
Prentice-Hall of India Private Limited, *New Delhi*
Prentice-Hall of Japan, Inc., *Tokyo*
Simon & Schuster Asia Pte. Ltd., *Singapore*
Editora Prentice-Hall do Brasil, Ltda., *Rio de Janeiro*

CONTENTS

TO THE STUDENT

The three-book series, ENGLISH SKILLS BY OBJECTIVES, is designed to help you develop the skills in English that you need to write effective sentences and paragraphs. To write well, you must first learn how the English language works. The structure of a language and how it works is called its grammar. The first book of this series, GRAMMAR FUNDAMENTALS, will introduce you to the different parts of the English language. You will learn how to identify the parts of speech and the parts of a sentence. A mastery of basic grammar skills will enable you to use these parts of language correctly and effectively in your writing.

The title of this series, ENGLISH SKILLS BY OBJECTIVES, means that, unlike some English books you may have used in the past, the material to be learned is broken into smaller "objectives" or goals for you to accomplish. The first book of this program consists of a Pretest, 9 Skill Units, and a Posttest.

Here's how the program works:

Pretest—Take the Pretest to find out what English skills you need to work on. Don't worry about the questions you don't know the answers to. This book will help you learn how to answer them. Check you answers in the separate Answer Key and then turn to the Skills Correlation Chart on pages 14 and 15 in the text. The chart lists the pages that have the information you will need to solve the questions you missed.

Skill Units—Each unit of the book, known as a Skill Unit, is divided into smaller units of learning called "Subskills." Since each Subskill focuses on a specific part of an English skill, it allows you to learn one bit of information at a time. You will always know what you are to learn and how you will learn it. Each Subskill begins with an objective explaining what activity you will be able to perform after you finish the Subskill. At the end of each Subskill, there is an EXERCISE for you to complete to see how well you understand the material. If you need additional practice, a SUPPLEMENTAL EXERCISE, which also contains a summary review of the Subskill, is provided. You can use these exercises for review at any time. At the end of each Skill Unit is a SELF-CHECK that allows you to check your understanding of all that you have learned in the unit. The SELF-CHECK has no time limit. This will enable you to think about each question and give the best possible answer.

Posttest—Take the Posttest to review your performance in all the skills in ENGLISH SKILLS BY OBJECTIVES, BOOK ONE.

Once you have mastered all the skills in Book One, you will then be ready to go on to ENGLISH SKILLS BY OBJECTIVES, BOOK TWO.

With this approach, you can build strong English skills. Take the time to work through ENGLISH SKILLS BY OBJECTIVES, BOOK ONE. You will make progress and the proof will be in your mastery of grammar fundamentals.

LIST OF ABBREVIATIONS

Adj	adjective
Adv	adverb
AV	action verb
DO	direct object
HV	helping verb
IO	indirect object
LV	linking verb
MV	main verb
N	noun
Prep phrase	prepositional phrase
Pro	pronoun
S	subject
SC	subject complement
V	verb

ENGLISH SKILLS BY OBJECTIVES

BOOK ONE

Pretest
GRAMMAR FUNDAMENTALS

Before you begin working on this book, take the following test. The test will help you find out how much you already know about grammar fundamentals. The test will also show you which parts of the book you should study most.

The test is divided into nine parts, one part for each unit in the book. You may want to take the test all at once or one unit at a time, depending on what you and your instructor decide. When you complete the test, check your answers in the Answer Key for Book One. Then turn to the Skills Correlation Chart on pages 14 and 15 and circle the numbers of any questions you missed. The chart will show you which parts of this book cover the English skills that gave you the most trouble. You should study the parts that match the questions that you missed on the test.

Skill Unit 1: Identifying Nouns

Part A. Underline all the nouns, or naming words, you find in the following sentences.

EXAMPLE: Give the <u>envelope</u> on the <u>table</u> to <u>Doug</u>.

1. The doctor told his patient to eat more fresh fruits and vegetables.

2. Are the housewares located in this part of the store?

3. Do your children ride a bus to school?

4. My grandmother still bakes five loaves of bread each morning.

Part B. Underline all the common nouns you find in the following sentences and capitalize all the proper nouns.

EXAMPLE: My <u>cousin</u> r̶uth from a̶lberta is in <u>town</u>.
                     R   A

5. On wednesday, louise visited the home of her good friend helen corbit.

6. My favorite holidays are christmas and easter.

7. Donald went back to work with his old employer, macon manufacturing company.

8. Is dr. ozawa going on vacation this august?

Part C. Some words serve as noun markers because they often come before common nouns. In the following sentences, circle the noun markers and underline the nouns.

EXAMPLE: (The) doctor is seeing (a) patient right now.

9. The woman was standing on the corner when the accident occurred.

10. The soldier was waiting outside the gate.

11. The children have not cleaned the bedroom in a week.

12. A dog was howling in the street last night.

Answers appear on page 1 in the Answer Key for Book One.

Skill Unit 2:   Identifying Pronouns

Part A. Underline all the personal pronouns you find in the following sentences.

EXAMPLE: Are <u>you</u> going to see <u>her</u> tonight?

1. We knew that you would be late for the meeting with the school principal.

2. He needed the key to the apartment they were renting.

3. Was she able to get it from them?

4. I never knew the people in the apartment next to me.

5. They never spoke to us in the hall.

Part B. Underline all the possessive pronouns you find in the following sentences.

EXAMPLE: Did he know the beer in the refrigerator was <u>yours</u>?

6. It's easy to guess why the kitten ran to its mother when the dog appeared.

7. Her aunt was in the hospital for several weeks when she broke her hip.

8. Your new boss seems to like the work you're doing.

9. My friend sold his motorcycle to your cousin, didn't he?

10. Our only complaint is that his music is sometimes too loud.

Part C. In each of the following sentences, underline all the interrogative, demonstrative, and indefinite pronouns you find. Then, rewrite them on the lines below each sentence and write interrogative, demonstrative, or indefinite after each pronoun to identify what type it is.

EXAMPLE: Where did everyone go?

Where—interrogative   everyone—indefinite

11. Whom do you think this belongs to?

12. Someone has left that sitting in my parking space for the last two days.

13. Would everyone please park in his or her own space?

14. Any of them will do.

15. Which of those are yours?

Answers appear on pages 1 and 2 in the Answer Key for Book One.

Skill Unit 3:   Identifying Action Verbs

Part A.   Underline all the action verbs you find in the following sentences.

EXAMPLE: Todd <u>found</u> his glasses under the couch.

1.   He reads the paper every day.

2.   I really like my new apartment.

3.   I see your sister in the market almost every week.

4.   We invited the Gentrys to dinner on Thursday.

Part B.   Underline the main verb and circle any helping verbs you find in the following sentences.

EXAMPLE: I (could)(have) <u>travelled</u> to Pittsburgh by train instead of by bus.

5.   I have been looking all over the house for the car keys.

6.   He had been waiting for almost two hours.

7.   They will have arrived by this time tomorrow.

8.   I should have given him the box.

Part C.   A sentence can have more than one verb. Underline all the verbs or verb phrases in the following sentences.

EXAMPLE: We <u>brought</u> our fishing rods but <u>forgot</u> the bait.

9.   The children ate breakfast, dressed, gathered their books, and left for school.

10.   Mark and Anne cleared the table and washed the dishes.

11.   We tucked the children into bed, kissed each one, turned the light off, and went downstairs.

12.   I see her almost every day but seldom speak to her.

Part D.   Verb phrases can be divided by other words in the sentence. Underline all the verbs and verb phrases in the following sentences. Do not underline words which are not part of the verb phrase.

EXAMPLE: <u>Did</u> you <u>see</u> Roberta at the party?

13.   Would you help me, Tony?

14.   I am only working until five today.

15. What do you think about that?

16. We will never finish this job before the end of the day.

Answers appear on page 2 in the Answer Key for Book One.

Skill Unit 4: Identifying Subject-Verb Combinations

Part A. Underline the subject of each sentence once and the verb twice.

EXAMPLE: After the game, <u>we</u> <u>ate</u> supper.

1. Everyone went to the amusement park.

2. During the storm, several trees fell across the road.

3. The festival lasted for three days.

4. The little girl smiled shyly.

Part B. A sentence may have more than one subject or verb. In each of the following sentences, underline the subjects once and the verbs twice. Then, circle the words that connect the compound subjects and compound verbs.

EXAMPLE: <u>Susan</u>(and)<u>I</u> <u>looked</u> for you(but)<u>could</u> not <u>find</u> you.

5. Neither Jason nor I want or need your help.

6. Did Robert or his sister find my hat?

7. The doctors and nurses worked around the clock.

8. Either my sister or my brother will live in my old apartment.

Part C. In each of the following sentences, underline the subject once and the verbs or verb phrases twice. If the subject is understood, write <u>you</u> in parentheses in the space after each sentence.

EXAMPLE: <u>Take</u> the money and <u>run</u>!   ___(you)___

9. Before each show, he turns out the lights and closes the doors to the auditorium. _____

10. Leave your muddy boots at the door. _____

11. Pass the salt and pepper, please. _____

12. The doctor just shook his head sadly. _____

Part D. Each of the following sentences has a subject-verb combination in inverted order. Underline the subject once and the verb or verb phrase twice.

EXAMPLE: When <u>is</u> the <u>repairman</u> <u>coming</u>?

13. Are we going to the ball game?

14. Here is today's newspaper.

15. In front of us lay the most dangerous adventure of all.

16. There will be about one hundred people at the church supper.

Part E. More complicated sentences may have more than one subject-verb combination. Find all the subject-verb combinations in the following sentences. Underline the subjects once and the verbs twice.

EXAMPLE: <u>I</u> <u>saw</u> Barry before <u>he</u> <u>went</u> on vacation.

17. We watched while the men completed the repairs on our house.

18. When the wind calmed, we opened the cellar door and looked out.

19. Whenever you need help, you can call me at home.

20. If you finish in the garage, you can start on the back porch.

Part F. Sometimes, words come between the subject and the verb in a sentence. See if you can find the subject-verb combinations in these sentences. Underline the subjects once and the verbs twice.

EXAMPLE: The <u>children</u> waving the red banners <u>are joining</u> the parade.

21. The woman in the straw hat would like some more iced tea.

22. The group of men carrying the injured miner hurried toward the waiting ambulance.

23. Persons already having tickets to the concert may enter the auditorium through the north door.

24. My friend without auto insurance has just had an accident.

Answers appear on pages 2 and 3 in the Answer Key for Book One.

Skill Unit 5:   Identifying Linking Verbs

Part A.   In the following sentences, the forms of the verb <u>be</u> are underlined. Decide if the form of <u>be</u> is used as a linking verb or if it is a helper for an action verb. If it is a linking verb, write <u>LV</u> in the blank and circle the word which renames the subject. If it is part of an action verb phrase, write <u>AV</u> in the blank.

EXAMPLE: They <u>were</u> the only (people) at the party without gifts.

                   __LV__

1. I <u>am</u> an excellent cook.   _____

2. My sister and her friend <u>are</u> going to the beach.   _____

3. My favorite story <u>is</u> *Gone With the Wind.*   _____

4. He <u>will</u> probably <u>be</u> a very rich man some day.   _____

5. We <u>were</u> watching the late movie when he called. _____

Part B.   In the following sentences, the forms of the verb <u>be</u> are underlined. Decide if the form of <u>be</u> is used as a linking verb or if it is used as a helper for an action verb. If it is a linking verb, write <u>LV</u> in the blank and circle the word or words which describe the subject. If the form of <u>be</u> is part of an action verb phrase, write <u>AV</u> in the blank.

EXAMPLE: <u>Are</u> you (mad) at Richard?   __LV__

6. She <u>is</u> very friendly.   _____

7. My aunt <u>is</u> coming to visit next week.   _____

8. My friend Robert <u>was</u> very tired after the match. _____

9. <u>Will</u> I <u>be</u> tall when I grow up?   _____

10. <u>Was</u> Mrs. Smith happy to receive the flowers?   _____

Part C.   The verbs in the following sentences have been underlined. Read each sentence carefully. Decide if the verb is used as a linking or as an action verb. If the verb is used as a linking verb, write <u>LV</u> in the blank and circle the word or words which describe the subject of the sentence. If the verb is used as an action verb, write <u>AV</u> in the blank.

EXAMPLE: These roses <u>smell</u> (wonderful.)   __LV__

11. I <u>smelled</u> the cookies from outside.   _____

12. <u>Did</u> you <u>taste</u> the corn?   _____

13. It <u>tastes</u> sweet and fresh. _____

14. I <u>feel</u> fine today. _____

15. He <u>felt</u> the hot stove with his hand. _____

Answers appear on pages 3 and 4 in the Answer Key for Book One.

Skill Unit 6: Identifying Adjectives

Part A. In a sentence, an adjective can answer the questions "What kind?", "How much?", "How many?", or "Which one?" about a noun or a pronoun. Find all the adjectives in each of the following sentences. Then, in the blank after each sentence, write the adjectives and the question each answers.

EXAMPLE: Put some ointment on that burn.

_____some—How much?_____that—Which one?_____

1. We have to drive down those steep, dangerous hills behind our house.

   _____

2. The calm and beautiful bay shimmered in the moonlight.

   _____

3. The chairman was the last person to enter the crowded room.

   _____

4. The morning was cold, so we made some coffee.

   _____

5. The three eager children ran toward the new playground.

   _____

Part B. Find all the adjectives in the following sentences. Underline them and draw an arrow to the word they describe.

EXAMPLE: Is your cousin <u>young</u> or <u>old</u>?

6. Our garden, sunny and quiet, is a pleasant place to relax.

7. That man is an excellent teacher.

8. My two sisters are tall and slender.

9. My work at the factory is difficult and boring.

10. Would you rather work in a large, busy office?

Answers appear on page 4 in the Answer Key for Book One.

Skill Unit 7:   Identifying Adverbs

Part A. In a sentence, an adverb can answer the question "How?", "Where?", or "When?" about an action verb. Underline the adverbs in the following sentences. After each sentence, write the question that has been answered by the adverb.

EXAMPLE: Come <u>here</u>!   <u>Where?</u>

1. Lin walked outside.   _____
2. The child cried loudly.   _____
3. He drove slowly past the house.   _____
4. I never wanted a dog.   _____

Part B. Write the adverbs that are formed from the following adjectives.

	Adjective	**Adverb**
EXAMPLE:	careless	carelessly
5.	slow	_____
6.	happy	_____
7.	possible	_____
8.	beautiful	_____

Part C. In each of the following pairs of sentences, a word is shown in two different positions. Put an X in the blank after each sentence in which the word acts as an adverb modifying a form of the verb <u>walk</u>. Sometimes, you will need to put an X in both blanks.

EXAMPLE: I <u>only</u> walked my dog for ten minutes.   <u>X</u>
          I walked <u>only</u> my dog and not my cat.   ____

9. We walked <u>slowly</u> around the block.   ____
   We walked around the block <u>slowly</u>.   ____

10. I <u>just</u> walked to town and back.   ____
    I walked <u>just</u> to town and no farther.   ____

11. Some people walk to work <u>quickly</u>. ____

Some people walk <u>quickly</u> to work. ____

12. <u>Usually</u>, we walk in the park after supper. ____

We <u>usually</u> walk in the park after supper. ____

Part D. Find all the adverbs in the following sentences. On the line that follows each sentence, write the adverbs and the word each adverb modifies.

EXAMPLE: The wind is blowing unusually hard.

<u>   unusually—hard   hard—is blowing   </u>

13. They walked very quickly past the supervisor's office.

_____

14. We ran into problems almost immediately.

_____

15. Too slowly, the door opened.

_____

16. It is extremely difficult to get good results.

_____

Answers appear on pages 4 and 5 in the Answer Key for Book One.

Skill Unit 8:   Identifying Prepositions and Conjunctions

Part A. Find all the prepositional phrases in each of the following sentences and circle them. Then, underline the preposition once and the object of the preposition twice.

EXAMPLE: Please turn (at the next <u>street</u>) and stop (<u>beside</u> the <u>entrance</u>.)

1. The village of Hampton lies just beyond those hills.

2. We were within fifteen miles of the airport.

3. I won't leave without you.

4.   He stood quietly behind the counter.

5.   The boys leaned lazily against the fence.

6.   The river flows through the town and down the valley.

7.   During the interview, he paced nervously between the chair and the desk.

8.   Put the letter into the envelope and place it on his desk.

Part B.   Underline the conjunction in each of the following sentences. Then, in the space following each sentence, tell whether the conjunction connects word to word, phrase to phrase, or statement to statement.

EXAMPLE: You should send a résumé <u>and</u> call for a job interview.

<u>   word to word   </u>

9.   Dress neatly and conservatively for the interview.

_____

10.   Arrive on time or before your appointment.

_____

11.   It's good to be well-informed about the type of work the company does, so you can make a good impression.

_____

12.   Find out something about the company by reading about it or by talking to an employee.

_____

13.   Be prepared to talk about your skills and experience.

_____

14.   Be neither too shy nor too aggressive.

_____

15.   Try to appear well-informed yet willing to learn more.

_____

16.   You should ask questions about the company, but it is usually wise to save most questions about benefits for a later time.

_____

Answers appear on page 5 in the Answer Key for Book One.

Skill Unit 9:   Identifying Simple Sentences

Part A.   In each of the following sentences, write S over each subject and V over each verb. If the subject is understood, write you in parentheses in the blank after the sentence.

             S V
EXAMPLE: I usually shop for groceries after work. _____

1. I rarely write to my mother. _____

2. Stop! _____

3. Do Li and David live in town? _____

4. You should eat and rest. _____

5. The man with the bushy mustache sat quietly in the corner.

_____

Part B.   In each of the following sentences, write S over each subject, V over each verb, and DO over each direct object. If the subject is understood, write you in parentheses in the blank after the sentence.

             V   DO
EXAMPLE: Give the money to Jim.   (you)

6. Could you help me with the groceries? _____

7. I heard my favorite song on the radio this morning. _____

8. Marion and Kim can help. _____

9. We washed the car and cut the grass on Saturday. _____

10. Get my purse from the car. _____

Part C.   In each of the following sentences, write S over each subject, V over each verb, DO over each direct object, and IO over each indirect object. If the subject is understood, write you in parentheses in the blank after the sentence.

             S   V   V IO   DO
EXAMPLE: The cashier did not give her the correct change. _____

11. I will need milk, eggs, cheese, and noodles. _____

12. Save me some pie. _____

13. I mailed Terry and Jean a package last Friday. _____

14. Did Aunt Maude and Uncle Clark send you a typewriter for your birthday? _____

15. The book is lying on the table in the bedroom. _____

Part D. In each of the following sentences, write S over each subject, V over each verb, DO over each direct object, IO over each indirect object, and SC over each subject complement. If the subject is understood, write you in parentheses in the blank after the sentence.

                    S V   SC
EXAMPLE: She is very attractive. _____

16. He is going to the store. _____

17. Ruth became a veterinarian. _____

18. Didn't you get my letter? _____

19. Art suddenly became withdrawn and sullen. _____

20. This food smells wonderful and tastes delicious. _____

Answers appear on pages 5 and 6 in the Answer Key for Book One.

Skills Correlation Chart for Pretest

After you check your answers, look at the following chart. Circle the number of each question you missed. Then study the subskill in which the skills for the questions you missed are explained.

		QUESTION NUMBER	SUBSKILL NUMBER	SUBSKILL NAME	PAGE NUMBER
Skill Unit One	IDENTIFYING NOUNS	1 2 3 4 5 6 7 8 9 10 11 12	1A 1B 1C	Identifying Words That Name Identifying Common and Proper Nouns Identifying Common Nouns Using Noun Markers	pages 17–21 pages 21–23 pages 23–26
		If you correctly answered 8 or fewer questions, you should study the subskills in Unit One for the questions you missed. *If you correctly answered 9 or more of the questions in Unit One, go to Skill Unit Two.*			
Skill Unit Two	IDENTIFYING PRONOUNS	1 2 3 4 5 6 7 8 9 10 11 12 13 14 15	2A 2B 2C	Identifying Personal Pronouns Identifying Possessive Pronouns Identifying Interrogative, Demonstrative, and Indefinite Pronouns	pages 29–34 pages 34–38 pages 39–42
		If you correctly answered 11 or fewer questions, you should study the subskills in Unit Two for the questions you missed. *If you correctly answered 12 or more of the questions in Unit Two, go to Skill Unit Three.*			
Skill Unit Three	IDENTIFYING ACTION VERBS	1 2 3 4 5 6 7 8 9 10 11 12 13 14 15 16	3A 3B 3C 3D	Identifying Action Verbs in Sentences Identifying Verb Phrases, Main Verbs, and Helping Verbs Identifying Compound Verbs Identifying the Verbs in a Divided Verb Phrase	pages 45–49 pages 50–52 pages 52–54 pages 54–55
		If you correctly answered 11 or fewer questions, you should study the subskills in Unit Three for the questions you missed. *If you correctly answered 12 or more of the questions in Unit Three, go to Skill Unit Four.*			
Skill Unit Four	IDENTIFYING SUBJECT-VERB COMBINATIONS	1 2 3 4 5 6 7 8 9 10 11 12 13 14 15 16 17 18 19 20 21 22 23 24	4A 4B 4C 4D 4E 4F	Locating Subjects and Verbs in Sentences Identifying Compound Subjects and Compound Verbs Identifying Understood Subjects Identifying Subject-Verb Combinations in Inverted Sentences Identifying Sentences That Contain More Than One Subject-Verb Combination Identifying Subject-Verb Combinations When Words Come Between the Subject and the Verb	pages 58–62 pages 62–65 pages 66–68 pages 68–71 pages 71–75 pages 75–78
		If you correctly answered 18 or fewer questions, you should study the subskills in Unit Four for the questions you missed. *If you correctly answered 19 or more of the questions in Unit Four, go to Skill Unit Five.*			
Skill Unit Five	IDENTIFYING LINKING VERBS	1 2 3 4 5 6 7 8 9 10 11 12 13 14 15	5A 5B 5C	Recognizing That a Linking Verb Can Link Subject to a Word That Renames the Subject Recognizing That a Linking Verb Can Link the Subject to a Describing Word Identifying Linking Verbs Other Than Be	pages 80–83 pages 83–85 pages 85–88
		If you correctly answered 11 or fewer questions, you should study the subskills in Unit Five for the questions you missed. *If you correctly answered 12 or more of the questions in Unit Five, go to Skill Unit Six.*			

		QUESTION NUMBER	SUBSKILL NUMBER	SUBSKILL NAME	PAGE NUMBER
Skill Unit Six	IDENTIFYING ADJECTIVES	1 2 3 4 5 6 7 8 9 10	6A 6B	Identifying the Use of Adjectives Identifying the Placement of Adjectives	pages 90–95 pages 95–98
		If you correctly answered 7 or fewer questions, you should study the subskills in Unit Six for the questions you missed. If you correctly answered 8 or more of the questions in Unit Six, go to Skill Unit Seven.			
Skill Unit Seven	IDENTIFYING ADVERBS	1 2 3 4 5 6 7 8 9 10 11 12 13 14 15 16	7A 7B 7C 7D	Identifying the Use of Adverbs to Describe Action Verbs Spelling Adverbs Correctly Identifying the Placement of Adverbs Identifying the Use of Adverbs to Describe Adjectives and Adverbs	pages 101–104 pages 104–108 pages 108–110 pages 110–115
		If you correctly answered 11 or fewer questions, you should study the subskills in Unit Seven for the questions you missed. If you correctly answered 12 or more of the questions in Unit Seven, go to Skill Unit Eight.			
Skill Unit Eight	IDENTIFYING PREPOSITIONS AND CONJUNCTIONS	1 2 3 4 5 6 7 8 9 10 11 12 13 14 15 16	8A 8B	Identifying the Use of Prepositions Identifying the Use of Conjunctions	pages 119–123 pages 123–127
		If you correctly answered 11 or fewer questions, you should study the subskills in Unit Eight for the questions you missed. If you correctly answered 12 or more of the questions in Unit Eight, go to Skill Unit Nine.			
Skill Unit Nine	IDENTIFYING SIMPLE SENTENCES	1 2 3 4 5 6 7 8 9 10 11 12 13 14 15 16 17 18 19 20	9A 9B 9C 9D	Identifying Subject + Action Verb Sentences Identifying Subject + Action Verb + Direct Object Sentences Identifying Subject + Action Verb + Indirect Object + Direct Object Sentences Identifying Subject + Linking Verb + Subject Complement Sentences	pages 131–137 pages 138–143 pages 143–151 pages 151–158
		If you correctly answered 15 or fewer questions, you should study the subskills in Unit Nine for the questions you missed. If you correctly answered 16 or more of the questions in Unit Nine, you are now ready for Book Two.			

Skill Unit 1
IDENTIFYING NOUNS

What Skills You Need to Begin: None

What Skills You Will Learn: When you complete this skill unit, you will be able to identify common and proper nouns, capitalize proper nouns, and recognize noun markers.

Why You Need These Skills: To be able to write well using correct grammar, you first must recognize the parts of speech and know what job each has in a sentence. Some words name; some show action; others describe. In this lesson you will learn to identify words that name. Words that name are called nouns.

How You Will Show What You Have Learned: You will do the Self-Check at the end of this unit on page 26. The Self-Check consists of a short paragraph and an exercise of 15 items. In each of the sentences that make up the paragraph, you will identify the common nouns and noun markers and capitalize the proper nouns. If you correctly capitalize 13 of 15 words and identify 25 of 31 common nouns and noun markers in the paragraph, you will have shown that you have mastered these skills.

If you feel that you have already mastered these skills, turn to the end of this unit and complete the Self-Check on page 26.

Subskill 1A: Identifying Words That Name

When you complete this subskill, you will be able to recognize words that name a person, place, or thing.

A word that names a person, place, or thing is called a noun. The word <u>noun</u> actually means <u>name.</u> But a noun is more than just a name like <u>Maria</u> or <u>Robert.</u> Any word that you use to name a person or place is a noun. Any word that you use to name a thing is a noun.

17

Some things are real objects, which you can touch. Other things are feelings or ideas, which you can think of or talk about, but cannot touch.

A noun may name a person:

man	John
friend	Julie
aunt	Maria
lawyer	Isaac

EXAMPLE: The <u>soldier</u> was wounded.

The word <u>soldier</u> names a person; therefore, it is a noun.

A noun may name a place:

street	Sunset Boulevard
state	Kentucky
office	Cambridge Book Company
city	Boston

EXAMPLE: The <u>city</u> was covered with snow.

The word <u>city</u> names a place; therefore, it is a noun.

A noun may name a thing that can be touched (an object):

magazine	*Newsweek*
car	Chevrolet
dog	Lassie
building	Yankee Stadium

EXAMPLE: The <u>desk</u> was dusty.

The word <u>desk</u> names a thing that can be touched; therefore, it is a noun.

A noun may name a thing that cannot be touched (a feeling or idea):

skill	questions
years	weight
knowledge	honesty
grammar	addition

EXAMPLES: We admired his <u>courage</u>.

The word <u>courage</u> names a feeling; therefore, it is a noun.

My <u>birthday</u> is in <u>January</u>.

The words <u>birthday</u> and <u>January</u> are both ideas; therefore, they are both nouns.

A noun that names one person, place, or thing is called a **singular** noun. A noun that names more than one person, place, or thing is called a **plural** noun. Plural nouns are usually formed by adding s or es to a singular noun.

SINGULAR NOUNS: idea   valley   church   box
PLURAL NOUNS: ideas   valleys   churches   boxes

Exercise for Subskill 1A

Read sentences 1–5 and do the following:
- Write all the nouns you find in each sentence.
- Write what is named by each noun: a person, place, or thing.

Review your work to be sure you have completed each step.
You should find a total of 13 nouns in the sentences.

EXAMPLE: Her children were not allowed to walk home alone.

        children—person   home—place

1. The television was damaged in the fire.

2. Tennis is a popular sport in England.

3. The family camped in a trailer.

4. John asked the man for a ride to town.

5. A test will be given on Tuesday.

Check your answers on page 7 in the Answer Key for Book One. If you correctly answered all 5 items, go to Subskill 1B. If not, do the Supplemental Exercise for Subskill 1A.

Supplemental Exercise for Subskill 1A

A word that names a person, place, or thing is called a noun. A noun names a person or a place: woman, Dr. Thomas, Toronto, country. A noun names an object, or a thing that can be touched: lawns, cat, water, sugar. A noun also names an idea or feeling, or a thing that cannot be touched: time, answer, miles, love. Nouns may be singular or plural.

Read the list of words below, and then do the following:

- If the word is a noun, write <u>N</u> in the column labeled <u>Part of Speech</u>.

- If the word is not a noun, write <u>X</u> in the column labeled <u>Part of Speech</u>.

- Then, for each word that is a noun, tell whether it is the name of a person, a place, or a thing, by putting a check in the correct column.

Review your work to be sure that you have completed each step.

		Part of Speech	Person	Place	Thing
EXAMPLE:	villages	N		√	
1.	children				
2.	Japan				
3.	slowly				
4.	motorcycles				
5.	month				
6.	Indiana				
7.	Vivian				
8.	patriotism				
9.	are				
10.	tooth				
11.	George Washington Bridge				
12.	streets				
13.	doctor				
14.	anger				
15.	tall				

Check your answers on page 7 in the Answer Key for Book One. If you correctly answered 12 of 15 items, go to Subskill 1B. If not, ask your instructor for help.

Subskill 1B: Identifying Common and Proper Nouns

When you complete this subskill, you will be able to recognize common and proper nouns.

Common Nouns

There are two types of nouns—common nouns and proper nouns. **A common noun names a kind of person, place, or thing.** Look at the common nouns that follow.

A KIND OF PERSON:	cowboy
	athlete
	politician
A KIND OF PLACE:	country
	park
	street
	state
A KIND OF THING:	movie
	dog
	book
	day

Each of the words listed above names a kind of person, place, or thing.

Proper Nouns

A proper noun names a particular person, place, or thing. A proper noun always begins with a capital letter. A proper noun is often made up of more than one word. Look at the following proper nouns that name particular people, places, or things.

A PARTICULAR PERSON:	Barbara Walters
	Joe Frazier
	Robert Redford
A PARTICULAR PLACE:	Africa
	Yellowstone National Park
	Washington Avenue

A PARTICULAR THING: *Star Wars*
Tuesday
Catcher in the Rye

Each of the proper nouns listed above names a particular person, place, or thing. For example, Joe Frazier is a particular athlete; Washington Avenue is a particular street; and *Star Wars* is a particular movie.

Exercise for Subskill 1B

Read sentences 1–5 and do the following:

- Underline the common nouns once.

- Underline the proper nouns twice.

- Capitalize the proper nouns.

Review your work to be sure that you have completed each step.

EXAMPLE: Joe and maria went to niagara falls for their vacation.

1. The largest city near my home is austin, texas.

2. Hector and his wife bought a buick.

3. Barbara traded her old motorcycle for a new honda.

4. The class visited the museum on wednesday.

5. The traffic on main street is moving slowly.

Check your answers on page 7 in the Answer Key for Book One. If you correctly answered all 5 items, go to Subskill 1C. If not, do the Supplemental Exercise for Subskill 1B.

Supplemental Exercise for Subskill 1B

There are two types of nouns—common nouns and proper nouns. A common noun names a kind of person, place, or thing. A proper noun names a particular person, place, or thing. Remember, a proper noun always begins with a capital letter.

Read the list of words on page 23 and do the following:

- If the word is a common noun, write <u>C</u> by the word and give a proper noun for it.

- If the word is a proper noun, write <u>P</u> by the word, and rewrite it using capital letters where they are needed.

- If the word is a proper noun, tell whether it names a particular person, a particular place, or a particular thing.

Review your work to be sure that you have completed each step.

EXAMPLES: football team   C   Washington Redskins

new jersey   P   New Jersey—particular place

1.   country   _____

2.   vietnam   _____

3.   tuesday   _____

4.   store   _____

5.   mississippi river   _____

6.   senator edward kennedy   _____

_____

7.   ocean   _____

8.   city   _____

9.   marine corps   _____

10.   car   _____

Check your answers on page 8 in the Answer Key for Book One. If you correctly answered 8 of 10 items, go to Subskill 1C. If not, ask your instructor for help.

Subskill 1C: Identifying Common Nouns Using Noun Markers

When you complete this subskill, you will be able to use noun markers to identify common nouns in sentences.

Common Nouns Used with Noun Markers

Now that you understand that the job of a noun is to name things, you are ready to learn a trick in recognizing common nouns in sentences. If a, an, or the comes before a word, that word is usually a common noun. A, an, and the are sometimes called **noun markers** because they tell you that a common noun will soon follow. In the following examples, the nouns are underlined:

The box was open.

A rock was thrown.

An apple dropped from the tree.

In each of these sentences the common noun is preceded by a noun marker. These noun markers, a, an, and the, indicate that a common noun follows. Sometimes one or more words come between the noun marker and the common noun. Look at the following sentences in which the noun markers are circled:

The green box was open.

A large rock was thrown.

A ripe apple dropped from the large tree.

In each of these sentences, a word comes between the noun marker and the common noun.

Common nouns are not always preceded by these markers, but when you see a, an, and the, you should realize that a common noun will soon follow.

Common Nouns Without Noun Markers

When noun markers are not used, and you are not sure if a word is a common noun, try adding the in front of the word. If the word still makes sense, it can be a common noun. Use this test on the following examples:

Snow in summer is rarely seen.

To determine which words can be common nouns, try the before each word.

the snow—Yes, this is a noun.

the in—This doesn't make sense.

the summer—Yes, this is a noun.

the is—This doesn't make sense.

the rarely—This doesn't make sense.

the seen—This doesn't make sense.

This sentence would still make sense if it read: The snow in the summer is rarely seen.

Monkeys live in jungles.

This sentence would still make sense if it read: The monkeys live in the jungles. The nouns in this sentence are monkeys and jungles.

Exercise for Subskill 1C

Read sentences 1–5 and do the following:

- Underline the common nouns once.
- Underline the proper nouns twice.
- Capitalize the proper nouns.
- Circle the noun markers.

Review your work to be sure that you have completed each step.

EXAMPLE: Rita took her children to (the) zoo last sunday.

1. Lake michigan is a part of the great lakes.
2. Acid and water should be added to the battery.
3. The league of women voters sponsored a debate.
4. Frank was given a ticket for parking illegally.
5. Fertilizer must be spread evenly on the lawn.

Check your answers on page 8 in the Answer Key for Book One. If you correctly answered all 5 items, go to the Self-Check. If not, do the Supplemental Exercise for Subskill 1C.

Supplemental Exercise for Subskill 1C

A, an, and the are sometimes called noun markers because they tell you that a common noun will soon follow. When these noun markers do not appear, the can be put before a word to check if it is a common noun.

Read sentences 1–5 on page 26 and do the following:

- Rewrite each sentence and capitalize any proper nouns.
- Underline the common nouns.
- Circle the noun markers.

When you have rewritten all of the sentences, review your work to be sure that you have completed each step for every sentence.

EXAMPLE: My friends mark and gina went to california and rented a cottage on the beach.

My friends Mark and Gina went to California and rented (a) cottage on (the) beach.

1. That movie stars humphrey bogart and ingrid bergman.

_____

_____

2. Recent research has found that diet is important in preventing cancer.

_____

_____

3. A hurricane is expected off the coast of florida.

_____

_____

4. Did sandy open an account at liberty national savings bank?

_____

_____

5. The money was raised at a dance in new york last february.

_____

_____

Check your answers on page 8 in the Answer Key for Book One. If you correctly answered 4 of 5 items, go to the Self-Check. If not, ask your instructor for help.

SELF-CHECK: SKILL UNIT 1

In the spaces provided, rewrite the following paragraph. For each sentence, do the following:

- Capitalize the proper nouns.
- Underline the common nouns.
- Circle the noun markers.

NOTE: Do not capitalize or underline the words she and it. These words are not nouns. You will learn about these words in Skill Unit 2.

When you have rewritten the paragraph, review your work to be sure that you have completed each step.

When rita harris moved from ohio to new york, she could not find a job. rita had been a clerk before she married. However, she had not worked in ten years. After a divorce, she had to look for a job again. Programs that retrain workers can help people like rita. The government runs programs in many cities. rita enrolled in a program in manhattan. She learned to write a resume, type, and use a microcomputer. But for rita, the best thing about the program was that it lasted only six weeks. In february, rita got a job with an insurance company— rogers & peals, inc.

_____

_____

_____

_____

_____

_____

_____

_____

_____

_____

_____

_____

_____

_____

Check your answers on page 8 in the Answer Key for Book One. If you have correctly capitalized 13 of 15 words and identified 25 of 31 common nouns and noun markers then you have shown that you have mastered these skills. If not, ask your instructor for help.

Skill Unit 2
IDENTIFYING PRONOUNS

What Skills You Need to Begin: You need to be able to identify nouns in sentences (Skill Unit 1).

What Skills You Will Learn: When you complete this skill unit, you will be able to identify pronouns. You will identify personal, possessive, interrogative, demonstrative, and indefinite pronouns.

Why You Need These Skills: In a football game, when a running back or some other member of the team gets tired, the coach sends in a substitute. In a sentence, a noun can get "tired," too. Since nouns can get used so often, we sometimes send in "substitutes," or "stand-ins," for them. A word that stands in for a noun is called a pronoun.

You remember that a noun is the name of some person, some place or some thing. If we used the name of some person or some thing repeatedly in speaking or writing, it would be very confusing. It would also be boring and awkward. That is why pronouns are so useful and so important to know about.

How You Will Show What You Have Learned: You will do the Self-Check at the end of this unit on pages 42–44. The Self-Check consists of 15 sentences. You must correctly identify the pronouns in each sentence. If you correctly answer 12 of 15 items, you will have shown that you have mastered these skills.

If you feel that you have already mastered these skills, turn to the end of this unit and complete the Self-Check on pages 42–44.

The Importance of Pronouns

Read the two groups of sentences that follow. See which group sounds better to you.

(1)   Mr. Henry gave Mr. Henry's workers a day off. Since the workers had passed the goverment inspection with a high score, Mr. Henry felt that the workers had earned a reward. Mr. Henry told the workers that the workers should take the afternoon off. Mr. Henry added that the workers should not forget to be back on the job by eight o'clock the next morning.

(2)   Mr. Henry gave <u>his</u> workers a day off. Since <u>they</u> had passed the government inspection with a high score, <u>he</u> felt that <u>they</u> had earned a reward. <u>He</u> told <u>them</u> that <u>they</u> should take the afternoon off. <u>He</u> added that <u>they</u> should not forget to be back on the job by eight o'clock the next morning.

In the second group of sentences, the underlined words are pronouns. The pronoun <u>he</u> stands in for the proper noun <u>Mr. Henry</u>. The pronoun <u>his</u> stands in for the possessive noun <u>Mr. Henry's</u>. The underlined pronouns <u>them</u> and <u>they</u> substitute for the common noun <u>workers</u>. Using these pronouns makes the second paragraph sound better.

Subskill 2A: Identifying Personal Pronouns

When you complete this subskill, you will be able to identify some types of personal pronouns. Other types are presented in Subskill 2B.

One kind of pronoun is called the personal pronoun. **Personal pronouns stand in for the name of a person or thing that is known.** In the examples in this unit, the pronouns are underlined.

Jack got married. <u>He</u> got married.

Jack and Tina got married. <u>They</u> got married.

Personal pronouns stand in for:

- the name of a person speaking, or a group that includes the speaker—called "first person"

- the name of a person or group being spoken to—called "second person"

- the name of a person or thing being spoken of—called "third person"

Personal pronouns can be singular or plural. Look at the following chart for a summary of the personal pronouns:

Personal Pronouns

	Singular	Plural
FIRST PERSON	I, me	we, us
SECOND PERSON	you	you
THIRD PERSON	he, him she, her it, it	they, them

First Person Pronouns

First person means that the pronoun stands in for the name of the person or persons doing the speaking. The first person singular pronouns are I and me. The first person plural pronouns are we and us. Look at these sentences:

> I am going to the movie.
> Some friends are going with us to the movie.

Second Person Pronouns

The second person pronoun is you. It stands in for the name of the person or persons being spoken to. You can stand in for one or more people.

> John, I want you to come here.   (You is singular.)
> Class, I want you to get to work now.   (You is plural.)

Third Person Pronouns

The third person pronouns stand in for persons, animals, or things being spoken about. The singular forms are he, she, it, him, and her. The plural forms are they and them. Look at these sentences:

> Frank gave Sally a ring. She liked it.

The pronoun she stands in for the singular noun Sally, a person. The pronoun it stands in for the singular noun ring, a thing.

> The roads are slippery. They have been slick for a week.

They, a third person plural pronoun, stands in for the plural noun roads. They and them can be used for either persons, animals, or things.

Exercise for Subskill 2A

Part A. Use the following chart to complete sentences 1–5. In each blank, write the pronoun that correctly completes each sentence.

Personal Pronouns	Singular	Plural
FIRST PERSON	I	we
SECOND PERSON	you	you
THIRD PERSON	he, she, it	they

EXAMPLE: Ken, please call the school.   Do __you__ have the number?

1. Karen bought a car. _____ needed to drive to and from work.

2. The boots were too small. _____ pinched Martha's toes.

3. Mark went to see a movie Saturday. _____ did not enjoy it.

4. Until Sarah and I ran into Ralph at the party, _____ were not having much fun.

5. The movie was a comedy. _____ was very funny.

Part B. Use the following chart to complete sentences 6–10. In each blank, write the pronoun that correctly completes each sentence.

Personal Pronouns	Singular	Plural
FIRST PERSON	me	us
SECOND PERSON	you	you
THIRD PERSON	him, her, it	them

EXAMPLE: Sharon and I called out to Lou, but he didn't hear __us__.

6. Where is my hat? I want to wear _____.

7. If they did a bad job, you should ask _____ to do the work again.

8. Lou and Sherry studied the directions, but could not understand

_____.

9. I gave the cashier a ten-dollar bill, but he didn't give _____ the right change.

10. When Angela called, I told _____ the news.

Part C.   In the following sentences, the personal pronouns are underlined. Use the charts in Parts A and B to help you decide whether the pronouns are first, second, or third person pronouns. Then do the following for each sentence:

- Write the pronouns in the first space following the sentences.

- In the second space, write 1 if the pronoun is a first person pronoun. Write 2 if the pronoun is a second person pronoun. Write 3 if the pronoun is a third person pronoun.

- In the third space, indicate whether the pronoun is singular or plural by writing S for singular or P for plural.

Review your work to be sure that you have completed each step.

EXAMPLE: He said that we should wait.

  a.   He   3   S

  b.   we   1   P

11.   John said, "I have too much work to do, Kathy. Will you help me?"

  a.   _____   _____   _____

  b.   _____   _____   _____

  c.   _____   _____   _____

12.   The work schedule is out of date. It has not been revised for a month.

  a.   _____   _____   _____

13.   When Mr. Stewart got sick, he sent us home for the rest of the day.

  a.   _____   _____   _____

  b.   _____   _____   _____

14.   Mrs. Montoya said, "Boys, I want you to go to sleep."

  a.   _____   _____   _____

15.   We asked them to leave.

  a.   _____   _____   _____

  b.   _____   _____   _____

Check your answers on page 9 in the Answer Key for Book One. If you correctly answered 12 of 15 items, go to Subskill 2B. If not, do the Supplemental Exercise for Subskill 2A.

Supplemental Exercise for Subskill 2A

Personal pronouns can be singular or plural. They can be first, second, or third person pronouns. Refer to this list of pronouns to complete the exercise.

FIRST PERSON SINGULAR:	I, me
FIRST PERSON PLURAL:	we, us
SECOND PERSON SINGULAR:	you
SECOND PERSON PLURAL:	you
THIRD PERSON SINGULAR:	he, she, it, him, her
THIRD PERSON PLURAL:	they, them

Read sentences 1–10 and do the following:

- Find the pronouns and underline them.
- Write each pronoun on the line below the sentence.
- After each pronoun, write 1 if it is first person, 2 if it is second person, or 3 if it is third person.
- Write S if the pronoun is singular.
- Write P if the pronoun is plural.

Review your work to be sure that you have completed each step.

EXAMPLE: Mr. Johnson had many problems, but he never spoke about them when I was around.

he—3 S   them—3 P   I—1 S

1. That pump does not work well. It needs a new gasket.

2. Those pumps do not work well. They need new gaskets.

3. Al's wife has a new job. She likes it.

4. Al and Marie want to move. They need a bigger apartment.

5. Carl will stop working at 12:00. He wants to eat.

6. George and Peter will stop working at 12:00. They want to eat.

_____

7. Whenever he looks at the plan, Mr. Rosas tells me to change it.

_____

8. Whenever they look at the plan, Mr. and Mrs. Rosas tell us to change it.

_____

9. I called you, Rosemary, but the line was busy.

_____

10. I called, but both of you were out.

_____

Check your answers on page 9 in the Answer Key for Book One. If you correctly answered 8 of 10 items, go to Subskill 2B. If not, ask your instructor for help.

Subskill 2B: Identifying Possessive Pronouns

When you complete this subskill, you will be able to identify possessive pronouns. You will also be able to tell the difference between contractions and possessive pronouns and use these forms correctly.

Possessive pronouns are forms of personal pronouns. They show ownership or possession. Possessive pronouns can be singular or plural. They have first person, second person, and third person forms. Study the following chart of possessive pronouns.

Possessive Pronouns

	Singular	Plural
FIRST PERSON	my, mine	our, ours
SECOND PERSON	your, yours	your, yours
THIRD PERSON	his her, hers its	their, theirs

Most nouns become possessive (show ownership) by adding an apostrophe (') and s. Look at these sentences:

That car belongs to Nina.

That is Nina's car.

That car is Nina's.

The apostrophe (') and s let us know that something belongs to Nina. Any noun that is followed by an apostrophe shows possession. Now look at these sentences:

That car belongs to her.

That is her car.

That car is hers.

Her and hers are the possessive forms of the pronoun she. They can both stand in for a possessive noun—in this case Nina's. Notice that the possessive pronouns her and hers do not contain apostrophes. Look back at the chart of possessive pronouns. You will see that none of the possessive pronouns contain apostrophes.

First Person Possessive Pronouns

The first person singular possessive pronouns are my and mine. The plural forms are our and ours. These pronouns are underlined in the following sentences.

My brother gave our mother a bouquet.

Marvin's car is larger than mine.

The Smiths' apartment is bigger than ours.

Notice that in the first sentence, my comes before brother, and our comes before mother. These two pronouns must always be used right before a noun. In the second and third sentences, mine and ours do not come before a noun. These pronouns should never be followed by a noun. They always stand alone.

Second Person Possessive Pronouns

The second person possessive pronouns are your and yours. The forms for both singular and plural are the same. Read the sentences on the following page to see how these pronouns are used.

May I borrow <u>your</u> camera?

I believe this book is <u>yours</u>.

Team, put <u>your</u> gear in the lockers.

Class, these books are <u>yours</u> to keep.

In the sentences above, <u>your</u> is used before the nouns <u>camera</u> and <u>gear</u>. The pronoun <u>your</u> must always be followed by a noun. The pronoun <u>yours</u>, on the other hand, always stands alone. It is never followed by a noun.

Third Person Possessive Pronouns

The third person singular possessive pronouns are <u>his</u>, <u>her</u>, <u>hers</u>, and <u>its</u>. The plural forms are <u>their</u> and <u>theirs</u>. The following sentences show how these possessive pronouns are used.

That is <u>his</u> coat. That coat is <u>his</u>.

That is <u>her</u> idea. That idea is <u>hers</u>.

The cat licked <u>its</u> fur.

That is <u>their</u> cat. That cat is <u>theirs</u>.

Notice that the pronoun <u>his</u> can be used before a noun or can stand alone. The pronouns <u>her</u> and <u>their</u> must come before a noun, but <u>hers</u> and <u>theirs</u> must stand alone. The pronoun <u>its</u> is always used before a noun.

Contractions

Possessive pronouns are often confused with certain contractions. A **contraction** is a shortened way of writing words that often appear together. It is made up of two words combined into one by leaving out letters.

TWO WORDS: it is   you are   they are

CONTRACTION: it's   you're   they're

Notice that in each contraction, the omitted letter or letters are replaced by an apostrophe ('). An apostrophe shows that a letter or letters have been left out. The contractions <u>it's</u>, <u>you're</u>, and <u>they're</u> are often used incorrectly as possessive pronouns.

POSSESSIVE PRONOUNS: its   your   yours   their   theirs

REMEMBER: Possessive pronouns never contain an apostrophe. Pronouns with apostrophes are always contractions. The apostrophe in a contraction shows where letters have been left out.

Look at the following sentence pairs. Notice how the contractions you're, it's, and they're can be replaced by the words you are, it is, and they are.

CONTRACTION: You're late. (You're = you are)

POSSESSIVE: Your leg is broken.

CONTRACTION: It's time to leave. (It's = it is)

POSSESSIVE: The dog ate its food.

CONTRACTION: They're sorry for the mistake. (They're = they are)

POSSESSIVE: Their toys are scattered.

When you are trying to decide whether to use the pronouns you're, it's, and they're, ask yourself whether you can substitute the words you are, it is, and they are. If so, use the contractions. If not, use the possessive pronouns your, its, and their.

Exercise for Subskill 2B

Use the following chart to complete this exercise. Read sentences 1–5 and fill in the blanks with the pronoun that best completes each sentence.

Possessive Pronouns	Singular	Plural
FIRST PERSON	my, mine	our, ours
SECOND PERSON	your, yours	your, yours
THIRD PERSON	his, her, hers, its	their, theirs

EXAMPLE: Yesterday, I went skiing and broke ___my___ leg.

1. I gave John's brother a new suit for _____ birthday.

2. You and Marie have the same type of car, but Marie's car is newer than _____.

3. That turkey has lost _____ tail feathers.

4. The Joneses said that _____ vacation was ruined by rain. The Smiths said that _____ had also been ruined by rain.

5. The mechanic told us that _____ car needed _____ engine overhauled.

Be sure that you have not put any apostrophes in the possessive forms of the pronouns. That means that you should have written its, not it's, and yours, ours, theirs, not your's, our's, or their's. Count your answer wrong if you put an apostrophe in any of the possessive pronoun forms.

Check your answers on page 9 in the Answer Key for Book One. If you correctly answered all 5 items, go to Subskill 2C. If not, do the Supplemental Exercise for Subskill 2B.

Supplemental Exercise for Subskill 2B

Review the chart of possessive pronouns on page 37. Notice again that pronouns do not use apostrophes. Then do the following exercise.

Read sentences 1–10. Fill in the blanks with the possessive pronoun or pronouns that best complete the sentence.

EXAMPLE: Donna and Sue left __their__ coats in the hall.

1.   John, since you forgot _____ pen, I'll lend you _____ .

2.   Joe said we could use _____ car, but we decided to use _____ own.

3.   Wagging _____ tail, the Great Dane bounded out to meet us.

4.   The Martins offered us _____ assistance when _____ house was damaged by fire.

5.   When my brothers borrowed _____ car, I had to take the bus to get to work.

6.   We live just down the street. You can see _____ house from here.

7.   Jerry, if that glove is _____ , please take it home with you.

8.   Bill gave _____ piece of cake to Sally, who had dropped _____ .

9.   The horse tapped _____ hoof on the ground three times.

10.   Although Grace was interviewed, she did not see _____ picture in the paper.

Check your answers on page 9 in the Answer Key for Book One. If you correctly answered 8 of 10 items, go to Subskill 2C. If not, ask your instructor for help.

Subskill 2C: Identifying Interrogative, Demonstrative, and Indefinite Pronouns

When you complete this subskill, you will be able to identify interrogative, demonstrative, and indefinite pronouns.

Interrogative Pronouns

When the words <u>who</u>, <u>whom</u>, <u>whose</u>, <u>which</u>, and <u>what</u> are used to ask questions, they are called **interrogative pronouns**. Generally, we don't know what noun or nouns an interrogative pronoun is standing in for until a question is answered. Look at these sentences:

QUESTION: <u>Who</u> is coming to the party?

ANSWER: <u>Leroy</u>, <u>Tom</u>, <u>Juana</u>, and <u>Alicia</u> are coming.

We find out in the answer that the pronoun <u>who</u> stands for <u>Leroy</u>, <u>Tom</u>, <u>Juana</u>, and <u>Alicia</u>.

QUESTION: Julio, <u>what</u> is the matter with you?

ANSWER: <u>I've bumped my big toe</u>.

The pronoun <u>what</u> stands for the answer <u>I've bumped my big toe</u>.

QUESTION: <u>Which</u> of these books is mine?

ANSWER: The <u>two red books</u> are yours.

The pronoun <u>which</u> stands for <u>two red books</u>.

Demonstrative Pronouns

Demonstrative pronouns are pronouns that point out a specific person or thing. There are four demonstrative pronouns. They are <u>this</u>, <u>that</u>, <u>these</u>, and <u>those</u>. <u>This</u> and <u>that</u> are singular and <u>these</u> and <u>those</u> are plural.

SINGULAR: <u>This</u> is my coat.   Is <u>that</u> your dog?

PLURAL: <u>These</u> are our coats.   Are <u>those</u> your dogs?

Indefinite Pronouns

Indefinite pronouns are pronouns that stand in for a person, place, or thing that is not definitely known. There are quite a few indefinite pronouns. Look at the underlined indefinite pronouns in the following sentences to see how some of them are used.

<u>Someone</u> left a package for you.

Has <u>anybody</u> seen my hat?

Give me <u>all</u> that you can get.

<u>Nothing</u> has been done to help her.

<u>One</u> is not enough.

<u>Everyone</u> will be here.

Now study the following chart of indefinite pronouns before trying the next exercise.

Indefinite Pronouns

Singular		Plural	Singular or Plural
other	nothing	both	all
another	anything	few	any
everybody	something	many	more
anybody	everything	others	most
nobody	each	several	none
somebody	either		some
one	neither		
anyone	little		
someone	much		
everyone	no one		

Exercise for Subskill 2C

The following sentences contain demonstrative pronouns, interrogative pronouns, and indefinite pronouns. For each sentence, do the following:

· Underline all the pronouns.

· Write each pronoun on the line below the sentence.

· Write <u>demonstrative</u>, <u>interrogative</u>, or <u>indefinite</u> next to each pronoun to identify the type of pronoun it is.

Review your work to be sure you have completed each step.

EXAMPLE: <u>Who</u> ate the last piece of cake?

　　　　　　Who—interrogative

1. Will somebody help Jane?

_____

2. That is not the book Sam ordered.

_____

3. Which of these do you like better?

_____

4. Give these to Anna.

_____

5. Everyone was sorry to see the movie end.

_____

6. Does this belong to you?

_____

7. Nothing was wrong with either of the appliances.

_____

8. Several of those on the table are broken.

_____

9. What did Tony say about the dented fender?

_____

10. This is my favorite part of the show.

_____

Check your answers on page 9 in the Answer Key for Book One. If you correctly answered 8 of 10 items, go to the Self-Check. If not, do the Supplemental Exercise for Subskill 2C.

Supplemental Exercise for Subskill 2C

Interrogative pronouns are used to ask questions. The noun that an interrogative pronoun stands in for is often not known until the question is answered. The interrogative pronouns are <u>who</u>, <u>whom</u>, <u>whose</u>, <u>which</u>, and <u>what</u>. Demonstrative pronouns point out specific persons or things. The demonstrative pronouns are <u>this</u>, <u>that</u>, <u>these</u>, and <u>those</u>. Indefinite pronouns stand in for persons, places, or things that are not definitely known. The chart on page 40 lists the most common indefinite pronouns.

Read sentences 1–10 on page 42. Fill in each blank with a pronoun from the following list. For each sentence, there will be one pronoun that best fits the meaning of the sentence. Do the exercise so that you use each pronoun only once.

INTERROGATIVE PRONOUNS: who, which, what

DEMONSTRATIVE PRONOUNS: this, these, those

INDEFINITE PRONOUNS: each, nothing, someone, everyone

The words in parentheses tell you the type of pronoun to use in each blank.

EXAMPLE: _____What_____ is the matter with Joe?   (interrogative)

1. _____ called you this afternoon, but she didn't leave a message.   (indefinite)

2. There was _____ we could do about the problem. (indefinite)

3. _____ is my new roommate.   (demonstrative)

4. _____ of these is mine?   (interrogative)

5. Our seats are here; _____ are your seats. (demonstrative)

6. _____ happened to the papers on my desk? (interrogative)

7. _____ are the programs I like best.   (demonstrative)

8. The teacher was pleased because almost _____ in the class passed the test.   (indefinite)

9. _____ is going to win the tennis match?   (interrogative)

10. _____ of the boys had a chance to play the game. (indefinite)

Check your answers on page 9 in the Answer Key for Book One. If you correctly answered 8 of 10 items, go to the Self-Check. If not, ask your instructor for help.

SELF-CHECK: SKILL UNIT 2

The following sentences contain examples of all the types of pronouns you have studied in this unit. For each sentence, do the following:

· Underline all the pronouns.

- Write each pronoun on the line below the sentence.
- Write <u>personal</u>, <u>possessive</u>, <u>demonstrative</u>, <u>interrogative</u>, or <u>indefinite</u> next to each pronoun to identify the type of pronoun it is.

Review your work to be sure you have completed each step.

EXAMPLE: <u>What</u> did <u>he</u> tell <u>your</u> brother?

_____What—interrogative, he—personal, your—possessive_____

1. He didn't do anything wrong.

    _____

2. Those are her shoes.

    _____

3. Which of these are yours?

    _____

4. Give both of the checks to them.

    _____

5. I will lend you mine.

    _____

6. Who took all of my pencils?

    _____

7. What is this?

    _____

8. Ours was better than theirs.

    _____

9. That is its only disadvantage.

    _____

10. They are expecting one of their children to visit.

    _____

11. Tell us if you need anything.

    _____

12.   Nobody told him the rules.

_____

13.   We didn't like either of the choices.

_____

14.   Everyone likes the new system because it makes the work easier.

_____

15.   Hand me the hammer.

_____

Check your answers on page 10 in the Answer Key for Book One. If you answered 12 of 15 items correctly, you have shown that you have mastered these skills. If not, ask your instructor for help.

Skill Unit 3
IDENTIFYING ACTION VERBS

What Skills You Need to Begin: You need to be able to identify nouns (Skill Unit 1) and pronouns (Skill Unit 2).

What Skills You Will Learn: When you complete this skill unit, you will be able to identify action verbs and action verb phrases in sentences. You will be able to identify main verbs and helping verbs. You will also be able to identify compound verbs and divided verb phrases.

Why You Need These Skills: A group of words must have a verb in order to be a sentence. To write correct, complete sentences, you need to recognize the kinds of work verbs can do in sentences.

How You Will Show What You Have Learned: You will take the Self-Check at the end of this unit on page 56. The Self-Check consists of 20 sentences. You must find all the verbs and verb phrases in the sentences. If you correctly find the verbs in at least 16 of 20 sentences, you will have shown that you have mastered these skills.

If you feel that you have already mastered these skills, turn to the end of this unit and complete the Self-Check on page 56.

Subskill 3A: Identifying Action Verbs in Sentences

When you complete this subskill, you will be able to identify action verbs in sentences. You will be able to define the terms <u>verb</u> and <u>action verb.</u>

Action Verbs

The **verb** in a sentence shows action or links nouns and pronouns to words that identify or describe them. In this unit you will study action verbs. Linking verbs are discussed in Skill Unit 5.

An action verb tells what a person or thing does, has done, or will do. Most verbs are action verbs. In the examples on the follow-

45

ing page, the action verbs are underlined twice.

John <u>runs</u>.   (The <u>person</u> is John. The action is <u>runs</u>.)

The horse <u>jumped</u> the ditch.   (The <u>thing</u> is the horse.
  The action is <u>jumped</u>.)

Your plan <u>worked</u>.   (The <u>thing</u> is the plan. The action
  is <u>worked</u>.)

Some action verbs show mental rather than physical action. When we think, some kind of action is going on in the brain. Words such as <u>think</u>, <u>imagine</u>, <u>understand</u>, <u>realize</u>, <u>believe</u>, <u>consider</u>, <u>forget</u>, <u>dream</u>, and <u>speculate</u> are action verbs.

I <u>believe</u> you.

He <u>understands</u> French.

The coach <u>considers</u> her team the best in the league.

In the skill unit on nouns, you learned about the noun markers <u>a</u>, <u>an</u>, and <u>the</u>. They are words that signal that a noun will soon follow. If you are unsure whether a word is a verb, there are also clues you can use to help you.

Clue 1:   If <u>he</u>, <u>she</u>, or <u>they</u> is put before a word and the two words together make sense, the word may be a verb. Look at these examples:

They <u>forget</u>.

They <u>bother</u> me.

They <u>advance</u> quickly.

He <u>walks</u> slowly.

She <u>reads</u> a lot.

He <u>makes</u> me angry.

Clue 2:   Decide whether <u>ing</u> can be added to the word, forming another word that makes sense. If it can, the word may be a verb. (NOTE: If a verb shows action that takes place in the past, you will not always be able to add <u>ing</u> to it.)
   We can test this clue by using it on the same words that we used in Clue 1.

forget + ing   =   forgetting

bother + ing   =   bothering

advance + ing = advancing

walks + ing   = walking

reads + ing   = reading

makes + ing   = making

Notice that the spelling of some words changes when ing is added to them. In the examples above, forgetting, advancing, walking, reading, and making all changed spelling in some way.

Since all of the words in the first column have an ing form, they may be used as verbs. That does not mean that they are always used as verbs. For example, think about the word walks. Walks has an ing form, walking. You can also say, "He walks." Therefore, walks may be a verb. However, compare these two sentences:

(1) The security guard walks his rounds.

(2) The walks are made of cement.

In sentence 1, walks is definitely a verb. It fits both of the clues, as well as expressing the action in the sentence. In sentence 2, however, walks is the name of something. The noun marker the also signals that walks is a noun in sentence 2.

Many words in the English language can do different kinds of work, depending upon how they are used in sentences. Compare the use of the underlined words in the following sentences.

I work at a grocery store.

The work I do is dull.

In the first example, work is a verb expressing action. In the second example, work is a noun naming something.

Joe and Helen run every morning.

Jerry hit the winning run in the bottom of the ninth.

In the first example, run is a verb expressing action. In the second example, run is a noun naming something.

They make doughnuts every Friday.

That make of engine has been discontinued.

In the first example, make is a verb expressing action. In the second example, make is a noun naming something.

Exercise for Subskill 3A

Part A. Use the clues you have just learned to help you decide whether the words in the following list can be verbs. Write V on the line after each word that can be used as a verb. Write X on the line after each word that cannot be used as a verb.

EXAMPLE: wonder   __V__

1. mud ____
2. much ____
3. throw ____
4. skill ____
5. blood ____
6. bleeds ____
7. sit ____
8. believes ____
9. belief ____
10. window ____

Part B. Underline the action verb in each sentence twice.

EXAMPLE: Sam and Anne <u>ran</u> around the track twice.

11. Carol works as a doctor.

12. She loves her work.

13. Wendy thought about the assignment.

14. They believe him.

15. He calls her every week.

16. John forgot the message.

17. She received two calls this morning.

18. They make the stew too spicy.

19. She rides her bike in the park.

20. The cats leaped off the counter.

Check your answers on page 10 in the Answer Key for Book One. If you correctly answered 15 of 20 items, go to Subskill 3B. If not, do the Supplemental Exercise for Subskill 3A.

Supplemental Exercise for Subskill 3A

Remember that an action verb tells what someone or something does, has done, or will do. Actions can be physical or mental.

The following clues can help you tell if a word may be a verb. (1) The word <u>she</u>, <u>he</u>, or <u>they</u> can be put before the word so that the two words together make sense. (2) The word can have <u>ing</u> added to it and still make sense. Remember that some words can be either nouns or verbs, depending on how they are used in sentences.

Part A.   Read the list of words below and do the following:

· On the line after the word, write <u>V</u> if the word can be used as a verb.

· Write <u>N</u> if the word can be used as a noun.

· Write both <u>N</u> and <u>V</u> if the word can be used as both a noun and a verb.

· Write <u>X</u> if the word cannot be used as either a noun or a verb.

EXAMPLES: drive ____<u>N V</u>____

much ____<u>X</u>____

1. apple _____   2. begins _____

3. bats _____   4. realize _____

5. truth _____   6. absolutely _____

7. proved _____   8. carry _____

9. from _____   10. walks _____

11. slide _____

Part B.   Read each sentence. Write <u>N</u> in the blank space next to the sentence if the underlined word is being used as a noun. Write <u>V</u> in the blank space next to the sentence if the underlined word is being used as a verb.

EXAMPLES: How did you <u>break</u> your arm? _<u>V</u>_

I'm going to the post office on my lunch <u>break</u>.   <u>N</u>

12. Mrs. Garcia decided to <u>run</u> for chairperson of the committee.

____

13. The athletes prepared for their <u>run</u>. ____

14. The arms control <u>talks</u> lasted three days. ____

15. Nadia always <u>talks</u> too much. ____

Check your answers on page 11 in the Answer Key for Book One. If you correctly answered 13 of 15 items, go to Subskill 3B. If not, ask your instructor for help.

Subskill 3B: Identifying Verb Phrases, Main Verbs, and Helping Verbs

When you complete this subskill, you will be able to define the terms verb phrase, main verb, and helping verb. You will be able to identify the helping verbs and the main verb in a verb phrase.

Verb Phrases

In some sentences, the verb consists of only one word. In other sentences, the verb consists of more than one word. **A verb phrase is a group of words used as a verb.** In the sentences that follow, the verbs and verb phrases are underlined. Compare the sentences to see the difference between a one-word verb and a verb phrase:

(1) Joe <u>jumped</u> over the stream. (one-word verb)

(2) Jane <u>has been jumping</u> rope for an hour. (verb phrase)

(3) The cat <u>ate</u> its food. (one-word verb)

(4) The cat <u>will</u> not <u>eat</u> its food. (verb phrase)

Main Verbs

The main verb is the word in a verb phrase that tells the specific kind of action that is going on. It is usually the last word in the phrase. In Sentence 2 above, the main verb is <u>jumping</u>. In sentence 4, the main verb is <u>eat</u>.

Helping Verbs

Helping verbs, sometimes called helpers, are words that are added to the main verb to make a verb phrase. One thing helpers do is help the verb tell when an action takes place.

The words listed below can all be helping verbs. Study the list and try to remember as many helping verbs as possible. You will need to recognize helping verbs throughout the rest of this unit.

Helping Verbs

be	have	shall	can	do
am	has	should	could	does
is	had	will	may	did
are		would	might	
was			must	
were				
been				

In the sentences below, the helping verbs are underlined once, and the main verb is underlined twice.

Sarah <u>is</u> <u>going</u> to the store now.

Sarah <u>has</u> <u>gone</u> to the store already.

Sarah <u>will</u> <u>go</u> to the store tomorrow.

She <u>may be</u> <u>going</u> to the store.

I <u>might</u> <u>go</u> with her.

I <u>can</u> <u>go</u> with her.

Do you see how the helpers change the meanings of these sentences?

Some sentences require a helping verb. A helping verb must always come before a verb that ends in <u>ing</u>.

DON'T SAY: Sarah going to the store.

SAY: Sarah <u>is</u> going to the store.

Verbs that end in <u>ing</u> are always used with one of the following helping verbs: <u>am</u>, <u>is</u>, <u>are</u>, <u>was</u>, <u>were</u>, <u>be</u>, or <u>been</u>.

Exercise for Subskill 3B

Find the verb phrases in the following sentences. Look for the group of words that tells what someone or something does, has done, or will do. Underline the main verbs twice and the helping verbs once.

EXAMPLE: Eileen <u>had been</u> <u>working</u> for seven hours without a break.

1. We have been traveling for a long time.
2. That engineer has worked sixteen hours today.
3. The dog is protecting its master.
4. Jane should go home early.
5. By evening, my family will have been gone for ten hours.
6. Bill was looking for you.
7. Rod has worn holes in all of his socks.
8. The team might be leaving on Monday.
9. Mrs. Wright should buy some new linoleum.
10. That senator will object to our project.

Check your answers on page 11 in the Answer Key for Book One.

If you have answered all 10 items correctly, go to Subskill 3C. If not, do the Supplemental Exercise for Subskill 3B.

Supplemental Exercise for Subskill 3B

Review the information about verb phrases on pages 50 and 51. Then do the following exercise.

Read the sentences below. For each sentence, do the following:

- Underline the verb phrase.
- Write MV above the main verb.
- Write HV above each helping verb.

Review your work to be sure you have completed each step.

EXAMPLE: Tom <u>will have found</u> the mail by now.
(HV HV MV above "will have found")

1. We will be arriving in Dallas at six o'clock.
2. Marianne should ask someone for advice.
3. They have broken another record.
4. That company might be hiring more workers soon.
5. The team certainly does play better without him.
6. The children had eaten all of the candy.
7. The manufacturers should have answered my letter immediately.
8. I am leaving for work now.
9. The boxers have been fighting for thirteen rounds.
10. Lois has lost a ten-dollar bill.

Check your answers on page 11 in the Answer Key for Book One. If you correctly identifed the main verb and helpers in 8 of 10 sentences, go to Subskill 3C. If not, ask your instructor for help.

Subskill 3C: Identifying Compound Verbs

When you complete this subskill, you will recognize sentences that contain compound verbs.

One Person or Thing Can Perform Different Actions

Sometimes a sentence shows that someone or something does more than one action or has a choice of more than one action. In that case, the sentence has a **compound verb.**

The children <u>laughed</u> and <u>shouted</u>.

The children in this sentence performed two actions: they laughed and shouted. The two actions are connected by the word <u>and</u>. This sentence contains a compound verb. A compound verb will usually have <u>and</u>, <u>or</u>, or <u>but</u> between the two verbs.

The children <u>have been laughing</u> and <u>shouting</u> all afternoon.

This sentence also shows two actions done by the children. It has a compound verb. The two verbs are <u>have been laughing</u> and <u>(have been) shouting</u>. Instead of one-word verbs, the verbs are verb phrases. Notice that the words <u>have been</u> are omitted from the second verb phrase. In a compound verb phrase, it is not necessary to rewrite the helping verbs in the second verb phrase.

You <u>can leave</u> or <u>stay</u>.

This sentence shows that one person has a choice of actions. The sentence has a compound verb. The two verbs are <u>can leave</u> and <u>stay</u>.

Sam <u>came</u> in the front door but <u>left</u> by the back door.

This sentence shows two actions done by Sam. It has a compound verb. The two verbs are <u>came</u> and <u>left</u>.

Apply what you have learned about compound verbs by doing the following exercise.

Exercise for Subskill 3C

Underline the compound verbs or compound verb phrases in the following sentences.

EXAMPLE: Louis <u>rode</u> the bus uptown and <u>met</u> Della at the restaurant.

1. George will mow the yard or trim the shrubbery.
2. The supervisor had been instructing the crew and inspecting the equipment before the accident.
3. The worker poured, set, and smoothed the concrete foundation.
4. The children argued all day long but behaved better at dinner.
5. Doctor Orr cleaned, stitched, and bandaged the wound.

Check your answers on pages 11 and 12 in the Answer Key for Book One. If you answered all 5 sentences correctly, go to Subskill 3D. If not, do the Supplemental Exercise for Subskill 3C.

Supplemental Exercise for Subskill 3C

Review the information about compound verbs on pages 52 and 53. Then do the following exercise.

Underline the compound verbs or compound verb phrases in the following sentences.

EXAMPLE: We <u>will go</u> to the movies and then <u>order</u> a pizza.

1. Henry has been running and lifting weights this afternoon.
2. She works slowly but does a good job.
3. I am turning left and heading down Main Street.
4. Fred remembered my name but forgot my phone number.
5. You can take it or leave it.

Check your answers on page 12 in the Answer Key for Book One. If you identified the verbs and verb phrases in all 5 sentences, go to Subskill 3D. If not, ask your instructor for help.

Subskill 3D: Identifying the Verbs in a Divided Verb Phrase

When you complete this subskill, you will recognize divided verb phrases in a sentence and be able to identify which words are part of the verb and which words are not.

In a **divided verb phrase**, the main verb is separated from its helpers by other words.

Those books <u>have</u> not <u>been lost</u> after all.

The word <u>not</u> is not a helper. It is not a part of the verb phrase.

This letter <u>has been</u> carelessly <u>written</u>.

The word <u>carelessly</u> is not a helper. It is not a part of the verb phrase.

<u>Are</u> you <u>going</u> home?

In questions, part of the verb phrase will come before the word that shows who or what is performing the action. If you change the question into a statement, you can find the parts of the verb phrase more easily:

You <u>are going</u> home.

You may want to review the list of helping verbs in Subskill 3B before you try the following exercise.

Exercise for Subskill 3D

Underline the verbs and verb phrases in the following sentences. Underline only helping verbs and main verbs. Do not underline any words that come between the helping verbs and the main verb.

EXAMPLE: <u>Did</u> you <u>visit</u> your cousin today?

1. Raymond could not handle more than one problem at a time.

2. Is Dave going to the football game?

3. Has Ellen been seeing a doctor?

4. I have frequently noticed that sign.

5. Have you ever driven on that highway?

Check your answers on page 12 in the Answer Key for Book One. If you correctly identified the verbs and verb phrases in all 5 sentences, go to the Self-Check. If not, do the Supplemental Exercise for Subskill 3D.

Supplemental Exercise for Subskill 3D

Review the information about divided verb phrases. Then do the following exercises.

Underline the verbs and verb phrases in the following sentences. Underline only main verbs and helping verbs. Do not underline any words that come between the main verb and the helping verbs.

EXAMPLE: I <u>have</u> not <u>told</u> my boss about the mistake.

1. I can never remember the words to that song.

2. Where are we going?

3. My parents will not arrive before evening.

4. Al has not really answered the question.

5. May I see you for a minute?

Check your answers on page 12 in the Answer Key for Book One. If you correctly identified the verbs and verb phrases in 4 of 5 sentences, go to the Self-Check. If not, ask your instructor for help.

SELF-CHECK: SKILL UNIT 3

Underline the verb or verb phrase in each sentence. Remember, if the sentence contains a verb phrase, do not underline any words that come between the main verb and the helping verbs. Some sentences contain compound verbs.

EXAMPLE: Brian <u>has eaten</u> all the cake.

1. Jeff has been looking for his dog all day.

2. Kim is singing in the shower and using all the hot water.

3. We went for a ride in the country.

4. Do you believe me now?

5. That swimmer has been breaking all kinds of world records lately.

6. Maria cut her finger with a knife.

7. I saw a robin outside in the yard.

8. Have you read or heard about that horrible accident?

9. By the end of the century, people will have learned a lot about computers.

10. The horse cleared all of the jumps and won first prize.

11. Bernie spilled his drink on the floor.

12. I have been seeing many robins this year.

13. I could not solve the mystery or understand the clues until the end of the movie.

14. Has Bob ever sung that type of music before?

15. She has been nervously waiting for your call.

16. Are they making new arrangements for our trip?

17. She will ask for a raise next week.

18. Have you forgotten the message?

19. Julio knew everyone in the room.

20. The cuts on Barbara's leg were oozing blood.

Check your answers on page 12 in the Answer Key for Book One. If you correctly answered 16 of 20 items, you have shown that you have mastered these skills. If not, ask your instructor for help.

Skill Unit 4
IDENTIFYING SUBJECT-VERB COMBINATIONS

What Skills You Need to Begin: You need to be able to identify nouns (Skill Unit 1), pronouns (Skill Unit 2), and action verbs (Skill Unit 3).

What Skills You Will Learn: After completing this skill unit, you will be able to identify subject-verb combinations in sentences. You will recognize that in some sentences the subject is understood and not actually stated. You will be able to recognize compound subjects and compound verbs. You will also recognize that some sentences contain more than one subject-verb combination.

Why You Need These Skills: Now that you can recognize nouns, pronouns, and action verbs, you need to know what a subject is. The subject of a sentence is as important as the verb. Put the two together, and you have the basic framework of an English sentence. If you say "flows," you aren't giving a complete thought. But if you say, "The river flows," you have expressed a complete idea. With both a subject and a verb, it is possible to say something about someone or something. Before you can write complete sentences you must first be able to recognize subject-verb combinations.

How You Will Show What You Have Learned: You will take the Self-Check at the end of this unit on page 78. The Self-Check contains 15 items. If you correctly identify the subject-verb combinations in 12 of 15 items, you have shown that you have mastered these skills. If you feel that you have already mastered these skills, turn to the end of this unit and complete the Self-Check on page 78.

Subskill 4A: Locating Subjects and Verbs in Sentences

When you complete this subskill, you will be able to locate subjects and verbs in sentences.

Subjects and Verbs

A sentence is a group of words that expresses a complete thought. Every sentence contains a subject and a verb. As you learned in Skill Unit 3, the verb expresses action or state of being. In this unit, you will learn about the subject. **The subject of the sentence tells you who or what is doing the action or being spoken about.** The subject of a sentence is usually a noun or pronoun. Remember that nouns name people, places, or things and that pronouns stand in for nouns. In the examples in this book, S = subject and V = verb.

S   V

My husband cooks eggs for breakfast.

Husband is a noun that tells who is doing the action. Cooks tells what the action is. Husband is the subject, and cooks is an action verb.

S V

The bird flew low.

Bird is a noun that names what was doing the action. Flew shows what the action was. Bird is the subject, and flew is an action verb.

S V

He worked rapidly.

He is a pronoun. You will remember that a pronoun stands in for a noun. Therefore, a pronoun can be used as a subject. Worked shows the action. He is the subject, and worked is an action verb.

Verbs as Aids to Locating Subjects

The best way to find the subject of a sentence is to find the verb first. After you find the verb, ask yourself, "Who or what does the action shown by the verb?"

To see how this works in finding the subject, look at this sentence.

The snake in the grass struck at me.

In the sentence, the only word that expresses an action is struck. Struck is the action verb.

Now, who or what <u>struck at me</u>? Certainly not <u>grass</u>. Even though <u>grass</u> is a noun, it did not do the striking. The subject has to be <u>snake</u>, because <u>snake</u> tells what <u>struck</u>. You know now that <u>snake struck</u> is the subject-verb combination of this sentence.

Study the explanation of the next example very carefully. It will show you how to use what you have learned so that you can find subject-verb combinations. Remember, to find the subject of the sentence, always find the verb first. You can do this by using some of the hints you learned in Skill Unit 3. Now look at the sentence.

The tall boy wearing the red shirt won the race.

Step 1: Find the verb. You will see three words that look as if they might express action: <u>wearing</u>, <u>won</u>, and <u>race</u>. But only one of them shows the action of the sentence.

    a. The word <u>wearing</u> does not show the action of the sentence. Although verbs have <u>ing</u> forms, you remember from Skill Unit 3 that you must use one of the helpers <u>am</u>, <u>was</u>, <u>is</u>, <u>are</u>, <u>were</u>, <u>be</u>, or <u>been</u> with the <u>ing</u> form to make a verb. When the <u>ing</u> form is used without a helper, it does not show action. It is a describing word. In the example, <u>wearing the red shirt</u> tells you which boy the sentence is about.

    b. <u>Race</u> cannot be the verb because it is being used as a noun. You know <u>race</u> is a noun because the noun marker <u>the</u> is placed before it.

    c. That leaves the word <u>won</u>. <u>Won</u> tells what happened in the sentence. It is the verb.

Step 2: Find the subject. Now ask who or what <u>won the race</u>. Four words are left to choose from: <u>tall</u>, <u>red</u>, <u>shirt</u>, and <u>boy</u>. Substitute each word for <u>who</u> or <u>what</u>.

    a. The <u>tall</u>? won the race. No.

    b. The <u>red</u>? won the race. No.

    c. The <u>shirt</u>? won the race. Hardly!

    d. The <u>boy</u>? won the race. Yes.

The subject-verb combination is <u>boy won</u>.

Apply what you have learned about using verbs to find the subjects of sentences by doing the following exercise.

Exercise for Subskill 4A

Below are two columns labeled <u>Subject</u> and <u>Verb or Verb Phrase</u>. Each sentence in the exercise contains one subject-verb combination. Read each sentence and do the following:

· Find the verb or verb phrase and write it in the second column.

· Read the sentence again, and find the subject by asking who or what is doing something. The answer to your question will be a noun or pronoun. Write this word in the first column.

When you complete the chart, review your work to be sure that you have completed each step.

	Subject	Verb or Verb Phrase
EXAMPLE:	pilot	landed
1.		
2.		
3.		
4.		
5.		
6.		
7.		
8.		
9.		
10.		

EXAMPLE: The pilot landed at the county airport.

1. Several explorers voyaged to the South Pole.
2. The children were playing outside.
3. The weary doctor has collapsed on the couch.
4. Three brave firefighters died in the fire.
5. In the morning, Howard will buy a newspaper.
6. The news carrier brought our newspaper after dark.
7. Fifteen men have been arrested by the police.
8. The violent earthquake destroyed the building.

9. Probably the huge dam will burst next.
10. The dancers relaxed after the show.

Check your answers on page 13 in the Answer Key for Book One. If you correctly identified all subjects and verbs, go to Subskill 4B. If not, do the Supplemental Exercise for Subskill 4A.

Supplemental Exercise for Subskill 4A

The subject of a sentence tells you who or what is doing the action or is being spoken about. Subjects of sentences are usually nouns or pronouns.

The best way to identify the subject of a sentence is to find the verb first. After you find the verb, ask yourself, "Who or what is doing, has done, or will do the action?"

The car with the rusty fender stopped at the corner.

The only word in the sentence that expresses action is <u>stopped</u>. Therefore, <u>stopped</u> is the verb.

Now, who or what <u>stopped</u>? Certainly not the <u>fender</u>. Even though <u>fender</u> is a noun, it does not tell what stopped. The subject has to be <u>car</u> because <u>car</u> tells what <u>stopped</u>. You know now that <u>car</u> is the subject of the sentence.

Use this same method to complete the following exercise.

Read sentences 1–10. From the list below, choose the word that will best complete the meaning of each sentence. Write the word in the blank provided. After the sentence, write <u>S</u> if the word is used as a subject and <u>V</u> if the word is used as a verb.

Cross out each word in the list as you use it. Each word will be used once.

| hurt | tornado | cheered | talked | secretary | ~~asked~~ |
| rushed | shivered | manager | students | increased | ~~documents~~ |

EXAMPLES: John ___asked___ me a question. __V__

The secret ___documents___ were stolen. __S__

1. Several _____ were sent to the principal's office. ____

2. Our _____ has supervised our department for ten years. ____

3. The awful suspense _____ with every hour. ____

4. The marching band _____ in the freezing rain. ____

5. My feet _____ from walking over the stony road. ____

6. The frightened boy _____ to his father. ____

7. The _____ destroyed the building. ____

8. Hank _____ to his boss about a raise. ____

9. The _____ filed the papers. ____

10. The fans in the stadium _____ with joy. ____

Check your answers on page 13 in the Answer Key for Book One. If you correctly answered 8 of 10 items, go to Subskill 4B. If not, ask your instructor for help.

Subskill 4B: Identifying Compound Subjects and Compound Verbs

When you complete this subskill, you will be able to recognize compound subjects and compound verbs in sentences.

In Skill Unit 3, you learned that a sentence may tell about more than one action done by the same person or thing. In that case, the sentence has a compound verb.

      S   V   V
Jack came home and cooked dinner.

A sentence may also tell about two or more subjects who do the same action. In that case, the sentence has a **compound subject**.

      S   S   V
Jack and Laurie came home.

A sentence may also tell about two or more subjects who do the same two or more actions. In that case, the sentence has a compound subject and a compound verb.

      S   S   V   V
Jack and Laurie came home and cooked dinner.

Compound subjects can be identified easily because they are usually connected by and, or, or nor. You remember from Skill Unit 3 that compound verbs are also connected by and, or, or nor. Look at these sentences to see the patterns of compound subjects and compound verbs.

Compound Subjects and Compound Verbs Joined by And

      S   S   V
The men and women played softball at the company picnic.

Who played? <u>Men and women</u>. <u>Men and women</u> is the compound subject.

S   S   V   V

The men and women ate and drank at the company picnic.

Who ate and drank? <u>Men and women</u>. <u>Men and women</u> is the compound subject. What did the men and women do? <u>Ate and drank</u>. <u>Ate and drank</u> is the compound verb.

S   S   S   V

Men, women, and children leaped from the burning building.

Who leaped? <u>Men, women, and children</u>. <u>Men, women, and children</u> is the compound subject.

Compound Subjects and Compound Verbs Joined by <u>Or</u> and <u>Nor</u>

When compound subjects are joined by <u>or</u>, the sentence tells that one subject or the other performs the action.

S   S   V

Either Tom or Harry will walk the dog.

Who will walk the dog? Either <u>Tom</u> or <u>Harry</u>. <u>Tom or Harry</u> is the compound subject.

When compound subjects are joined by <u>nor</u>, the sentence tells that neither subject performs the action.

S   S   V

Neither Tom nor Harry will walk the dog.

Who will walk the dog? Neither <u>Tom</u> nor <u>Harry</u>. <u>Tom nor Harry</u> is the compound subject.

When compound verbs are joined by <u>or</u>, the sentence tells that the subject performs one action or the other.

S   V   V   V

Harry will either walk the dog or wash the dishes.

What will Harry do? He will either <u>walk</u> or <u>wash</u>. <u>Will walk or wash</u> is the compound verb.

When compound verbs are joined by <u>nor</u>, the sentence tells that the subject does not perform either action.

S   V   V   V

Harry will neither walk the dog nor wash the dishes.

What will Harry do? Neither <u>walk</u> nor <u>wash</u>. <u>Will walk nor wash</u> is the compound verb.

Exercise for Subskill 4B

Below are two columns labeled <u>Subject</u> and <u>Verb or Verb Phrase</u>. Carefully read each sentence and then do the following:

- Find and write down the verb or verbs. When you write a compound verb, include the connecting word as part of the verb.

- Find and write down the subject or subjects. When you write a compound subject, include the connecting word as part of the subject.

When you have completed the chart, review your work to be sure that you have completed each step.

	Subject	Verb or Verb Phrase
EXAMPLE:	soldiers and sailors	lived and worked
1.		
2.		
3.		
4.		
5.		

EXAMPLE: During the disaster, the soldiers and sailors lived and worked together.

1. Horses and mules pulled the boats on the Erie Canal.
2. Either Tom or I will attend the State Fair.
3. The speaker presented and explained the problem.
4. Tom and Ed washed and waxed the floors.
5. Neither biology nor geography will be offered next semester.

Check your answers on page 13 in the Answer Key for Book One. If you correctly answered all 5 items, go to Subskill 4C. If not, do the Supplemental Exercise for Subskill 4B.

Supplemental Exercise for Subskill 4B

A subject-verb combination may be made up of more than one subject and more than one verb.

```
  S       S     V    V
```
Tim and Cindy played and sang with the band.

The action words played and sang are verbs joined by and. Who played and sang? Tim and Cindy. Tim and Cindy is the compound subject. What did Tim and Cindy do? Played and sang. Played and sang is the compound verb.

Apply what you have learned about compound subjects and verbs by completing this exercise.

Below are two columns labeled Subject and Verb or Verb phrase. Carefully read each sentence and then do the following:

- Find and write down the verb or verbs. When you write a compound verb, include the connecting word as part of the verb.

- Find and write down the subject or subjects. When you write a compound subject, include the connecting word as part of the subject.

When you complete the chart, review your work to be sure that you have completed each step.

	Subject	Verb or Verb Phrase
EXAMPLE:	dog and cat	fought
1.		
2.		
3.		
4.		
5.		

EXAMPLE: My dog and cat fought all day.

1. A coat and an umbrella are hanging in the closet.
2. Carrie, Amie, and Carolyn revised the schedule.
3. Al took the test and passed it.
4. Bill and the other applicants waited two hours for their interviews and then left in disgust.
5. Sharon and I use cream in our coffee.

Check your answers on page 14 in the Answer Key for Book One. If you correctly answered 4 of 5 items, go to Subskill 4C. If not, ask your instructor for help.

Subskill 4C: Identifying Understood Subjects

When you complete this subskill, you will recognize that in some sentences the subject is understood and not actually stated in the sentence.

In some sentences, the subject is missing. How do we explain this when a sentence must always have a subject? The answer is that the subject is understood to be there. This happens when the sentence is a command or a request.

Stop! is a sentence. It gives a command. Who is supposed to stop? You, the person being spoken to. You is understood to be a part of the sentence even though it is not actually written or spoken.

Give me that gun!

The meaning is "You give me that gun!" The subject you is understood.

Help me!

The meaning is "You help me!" The subject you is understood.

Check your understanding of understood subjects by completing this exercise.

Exercise for Subskill 4C

Below are two columns labeled Subject and Verb or Verb Phrase. Carefully read the sentences on page 67 and do the following:

- Write the verbs in the second column.

- Write the subjects in the first column.

- If the subject you is understood, write the word you in parentheses: (you).

Remember, some subjects are stated and some are understood. When you complete the chart, review your work to be sure that you have completed each step.

	Subject	Verb or Verb Phrase
EXAMPLE:	(you)	give
1.		
2.		
3.		
4.		
5.		

EXAMPLE: Please give me another cup of coffee.

1. Halt!
2. They watched the sunset over the river.
3. Please keep out of my way.
4. Run to the store and get me a newspaper, please.
5. She put the money in her pocket.

Check your answers on page 14 in the Answer Key for Book One. If you correctly identified all of the subjects and verbs, go to Subskill 4D. If not, do the Supplemental Exercise for Subskill 4C.

Supplemental Exercise for Subskill 4C

Sentences that make commands or requests begin with a verb. The subject is understood to be the person to whom we are talking.

Wait just a second.

Wait is the verb. You is the understood subject.

Ask the mechanic for an estimate.

Ask is the verb. You is the understood subject.

Below are two columns labeled Subject and Verb or Verb Phrase. Carefully read sentences 1–5 and do the following:

. Write the verbs in the second column.

. Write the subjects in the first column.

. If the subject you is understood, write the word you in parentheses: (you).

Remember, some subjects are stated and some are understood. When you complete the chart, review your work to be sure that you have completed each step.

	Subject	Verb or Verb Phrase
EXAMPLE:	(you)	tell
1.		
2.		
3.		
4.		
5.		

EXAMPLE: Tell me about your discussion at the meeting.

1. The cars come and go all day long.
2. Meet me at the club at nine o'clock.
3. Go to the first red light and turn left.

4. She and I were listening to the radio.
5. Hold on to the rope.

Check your answers on page 14 in the Answer Key for Book One. If you correctly identified all of the subjects and verbs, go to Subskill 4D. If not, ask your instructor for help.

Subskill 4D: Identifying Subject-Verb Combinations in Inverted Sentences

When you complete this subskill, you will be able to recognize subject-verb combinations in sentences that do not follow the usual order.

Subject-Verb Combinations in Questions

In the normal pattern of an English sentence, the verb follows the subject. Sometimes this pattern is changed, however, and the verb or part of the verb comes before the subject. Then, we say the sentence is **inverted,** or in reversed order.

<pre>
  V   S   V
Are you going to the store now?
</pre>

The verb is divided by the subject in this sentence. To find the subject in a question, turn the question into a statement.

<pre>
  S   V
You are going to the store now.
</pre>

<pre>
  V   S   V
Has Tony called you yet?
</pre>

Turn the question into a statement to find the subject.

<pre>
  S   V
Tony has called you yet.
</pre>

Subject-Verb Combinations in Sentences That Begin with <u>Here</u> or <u>There</u>

<u>There</u> and <u>here</u> are never subjects. Sentences beginning with <u>there</u> and <u>here</u> should be rearranged into normal sentence patterns to aid in finding the subject. Look at the following examples.

       V   S
Here is your book.

The word here is not a noun or pronoun. It cannot be a subject. In sentences beginning with here and there, we can usually rearrange the sentence into a normal sentence pattern.

       S V
Your book is here.

Here's a more difficult one:

       V   S
There came the sound of footsteps on the squeaky stairs.

The word there is not a noun or a pronoun. It cannot be a subject. In this sentence, leave out there and rearrange the sentence into a normal sentence order. The verb is came. What came? The sound came.

       S   V
The sound of footsteps came on the squeaky stairs.

Subject-Verb Combinations at the End of Sentences

Usually subject-verb combinations are found at the beginning of a sentence. Sometimes, however, the subject-verb combination is found toward the end of a sentence. In some of these sentences, the verb comes before the subject.

Out in a distant valley far from civilization lived a fur trapper.

You can see that the best way to find the subject in a sentence like this is to find the verb first. Look for the action. Lived is the only word that expresses action. Then ask who or what performed the action. Who lived? The answer is trapper. Trapper is the subject.
You could turn this sentence around to read as follows:

       S   V
A fur trapper lived out in a distant valley far from civilization.

Out the door raced the frightened child.

Look for the verb. Raced shows action; therefore, it is the verb. Who raced? The child. Child is the subject of this sentence.
Once again, you can rearrange the sentence into a normal pattern.

       S   V
The frightened child raced out the door.

In this order, you can see more easily that child is the subject and raced is the verb.

To practice your skill in recognizing subject-verb combinations in inverted sentences, complete the following exercise.

Exercise for Subskill 4D

Rewrite each of the inverted sentences into a normal pattern. Underline the subject once and the verb twice.

EXAMPLE: Asleep on the bed was a small child.

A small <u>child</u> <u>was</u> asleep on the bed.

1. Are people leaving the city and moving to the suburbs?

    _____

2. Here are my hat and shoes.

    _____

3. Did Mrs. Peters sell her rug?

    _____

4. There go Joyce and Dwayne to the movies.

    _____

5. Across the street and down one block lives Ms. Haskins.

    _____

Check your answers on page 14 in the Answer Key for Book One. If you correctly rewrote all 5 sentences and identified all of the subject-verb combinations, go to Subskill 4E. If not, do the Supplemental Exercise for Subskill 4D.

Supplemental Exercise for Subskill 4D

The normal pattern of an English sentence starts with the subject followed by the verb. This pattern changes:

(1)   when a question is being asked

(2)   when the sentence begins with <u>here</u> or <u>there</u>

(3)   when subject-verb combinations come at the end of the sentence

V S   V
Is Sally attending the wedding?

V   V   S
There will be a reception at the restaurant.

V   S

Here is the invitation.

V   S

Down the long aisle walked the bride.

Check your understanding of inverted sentences by completing this exercise.

Rewrite each of these sentences into a normal sentence pattern. Then underline the subject once and the verb twice.

EXAMPLE: Have you seen my dog?

You have seen my dog.

1. Under this oak tree ran two squirrels.

   _____

2. Were you watching me?

   _____

3. There will be a huge crowd at the parade tomorrow.

   _____

   _____

4. Have Jenny and Roberto set a date for their wedding?

   _____

   _____

5. Into the yard dashed the eager dog.

   _____

Check your answers on page 15 in the Answer Key for Book One. If you correctly rewrote and identified subject-verb combinations in 4 of 5 sentences, go to Subskill 4E. If not, ask your instructor for help.

Subskill 4E: Identifying Sentences That Contain More Than One Subject-Verb Combination

When you complete this subskill, you will be able to identify the subjects and verbs in sentences that contain more than one subject-verb combination.

Sentences with Only One Subject-Verb Combination

So far, all of the sentences you have studied in this unit have contained only one subject-verb combination.

You have studied sentences in which one subject combined with one verb:

    S   V
    Herb bowled a perfect game.

You have studied sentences in which one subject combined with two or more verbs:

    S   V   V
    Herb bowled a perfect game and celebrated afterwards.

You have studied sentences in which two or more subjects combined with one verb:

    S   S   V
    Herb and his buddy bowled perfect games.

You have studied sentences in which two or more subjects combined with two or more verbs:

    S   S   V   V
    Herb and his buddy bowled perfect games and celebrated afterwards.

In all of the four sentences you have just read, there is only one subject-verb combination because each part of the subject combines with each part of the verb. The subjects share the same verbs.

Sentences with More Than One Subject-Verb Combination

Compare the following sentences:

    S   S   V   V
    Herb and his buddy bowled perfect games and celebrated afterwards.

    S   V   S   V
    Herb bowled a perfect game, and his buddy congratulated him.

Each sentence contains two subjects and two verbs. In the first sentence, however, the two subjects share the two verbs. There is only one subject-verb combination. In the second sentence, on the other hand, the two subjects do not share the two verbs. Who bowled a perfect game? Only Herb. Who congratulated him? Only his buddy. The second sentence contains two separate subject-verb combinations joined by the word and:

S   V   S   V

Herb bowled   and   buddy congratulated

Two or more subject-verb combinations can also be joined by but or or:

S   V   S   V   V

Herb bowled a perfect game, but his buddy did not believe him.

S   V   S   V

Herb must bowl another perfect game, or his buddy will never

V

believe him.

Here is another kind of sentence that contains more than one subject-verb combination. Can you find the combinations?

Although Martha called him, John did not come.

Step 1: First, find the verbs. The sentence contains two action verbs: called and did come.

Step 2: Now find the subject of the verb called. Ask yourself, "Who or what called?" The answer is Martha. Martha is the subject and called is the verb of the first subject-verb combination.

Step 3: Then ask, "Who or what did (not) come?" The answer is John. John is the subject and did (not) come is the verb of the second subject-verb combination. The word not is put in parentheses because it is not a helping verb. It is a describing word which makes the verb come negative.

The sentence contains two subject-verb combinations:

S   V   S   V   V

Martha called   John did (not) come

The rain fell so fast that it flooded the town.

Step 1: The action verbs are fell and flooded.

Step 2: Ask, "Who or what fell?" The answer is rain. Rain fell is the first subject-verb combination.

Step 3: Then ask, "What flooded?" The answer is it. In this sentence, it is a pronoun that stands for rain, but it, not rain, is the subject of flooded.

Check your understanding by completing the following exercise.

Exercise for Subskill 4E

Read each of these sentences. In the spaces provided, write the subject-verb combinations contained in each sentence.

EXAMPLE: As Bernie boarded the plane, Blanche waved goodbye.

<u>   Bernie boarded   Blanche waved   </u>

1. Although the doctor examined the patient, she could find nothing wrong with him.

   _____

2. After you read the menu, we will place our order with the waitress.

   _____

3. Mary dried the dishes, and I put them away.

   _____

4. Andrew would like a new car, but the new models cost too much.

   _____

5. The painter painted the house while the electrician fixed the wiring.

   _____

Check your answers on page 15 in the Answer Key for Book One. If you correctly identified the subject-verb combinations in all 5 sentences, go to Subskill 4F. If not, do the Supplemental Exercise for Subskill 4E.

Supplemental Exercise for Subskill 4E

Some sentences contain two or more subject-verb combinations. To find these combinations, use the same method used to identify one combination.

> The entire team was invited, but only three players went to the dinner.

This sentence contains two verbs, <u>was invited</u> and <u>went</u>. Ask yourself, "Who was invited?" The answer is <u>team</u>. The first subject-verb combination is <u>team was invited</u>. Now ask, "Who or what went?" The answer is <u>players</u>. <u>Players went</u> is the second subject-verb combination.

<pre>   S   V   S   V
When Alex heard the thunder, he ran for the shed.

       S   V   S   V
Mr. Jones likes cake, but Mrs. Jones prefers fruit.

      S   V   S   V
Lee filled the glasses with ice, Alice added the lemon, and

    S   V
Larry poured the tea.
</pre>

Apply what you have learned by completing the following exercise.

Read sentences 1–5. Underline the verbs or verb phrases twice. Underline the subjects once.

EXAMPLE: As the <u>band</u> <u>played</u>, the <u>audience</u> <u>talked</u> and the <u>television</u> <u>blared</u>.

1. Mother will sing, Bonnie will dance, and Susan will play the piano while the entire audience watches.
2. After Lou finished his chores, he read the newspaper.
3. Did you see George there, or had he left earlier?
4. The driver swerved to miss the car, but he hit another car anyway.
5. I was late for work because I missed the bus.

Check your answers on page 15 in the Answer Key for Book One. If you correctly identified the subject-verb combinations in 4 of 5 sentences, go to Subskill 4F. If not, ask your instructor for help.

Subskill 4F: Identifying Subject-Verb Combinations When Words Come Between the Subject and the Verb

When you complete this subskill, you will be able to recognize subject-verb combinations when words come between the subject and the verb.

Often a word or a group of words comes between the subject and the verb. These words often describe the subject. They can make it hard to recognize the subject and the verb of the sentence. In these sentences, you can identify the subjects and verbs if you continue to look for the verb first and then ask who or what does the action shown by the verb. Just ignore the words that come between the subject and the verb.

Look at the following example:

The man wearing the tan jacket screamed for help.

Step 1: What word expresses the action or tells what happened in the sentence? The answer is screamed. The word wearing is sometimes a verb, but it is not the verb in this sentence. It does not tell what happened. The words wearing the tan jacket are describing words. They describe the man.

Step 2: To find the subject, ask, "Who screamed?" The answer is the man. Man is the subject of the sentence.

S   V

The man wearing the tan jacket screamed for help.

Now look at this example:

The man was wearing a tan jacket.

Step 1: What word or words express the action or tell what happened in the sentence? The answer is was wearing. In this sentence, was wearing is an action verb phrase. Remember that when ing words are used as verbs, they need a helper before them. The helper in this sentence is was.

Step 2: To find the subject, ask "Who was wearing?" The answer is the man. Man is the subject of the sentence.

The words that come between the subject and the verb are not always ing words. Look at this example:

The eggs in the carton broke on the way home.

Step 1: Find the verb. Which word expresses the action? The answer is broke. Broke is the verb.

Step 2: Now find the subject by asking, "What broke?" The answer is eggs. Eggs is the subject. Carton is a noun, but it is not the subject. The carton did not break. The eggs broke. The words in the carton describe the eggs.

Here is another example:

Everyone in my family wears glasses.

Step 1:   Find the verb. Which word expresses the action? The answer is <u>wears</u>. <u>Wears</u> is the verb.

Step 2:   Now find the subject by asking, "Who wears glasses?" Look at the sentence carefully before you answer. The answer is <u>everyone</u>. <u>Everyone</u> is the subject. The words <u>in my family</u> describe <u>everyone</u>.

Apply what you have learned by doing the following exercise.

Exercise for Subskill 4F

Read each sentence. Underline the subject or subjects once and the verb or verb phrases twice.

EXAMPLE: The <u>woman</u> driving the red car <u>did</u> not <u>stop</u> at the light.

1.   The words of that song make me sad.
2.   That man using the potter's wheel is making a vase.
3.   The thundering herd of horses in the valley was running directly toward me.
4.   The herd of wild horses was thundering across the range.
5.   Someone in the audience laughed throughout the play.

Check your answers on page 15 in the Answer Key for Book One. If you correctly identified all of the subject-verb combinations, go to the Self-Check. If not, to the Supplemental Exercise for Subskill 4F.

Supplemental Exercise for Subskill 4F

Words that describe the subject often come between the subject and the verb. This can make finding the subject-verb combination tough. To make the job easier, ask yourself, "What is the action?" Then ask, "Who or what is doing this action?" Answers to these questions give you the subject-verb combination. Now, check your understanding by completing the following exercise.

In sentences 1–5, underline the subjects once and the verb twice.

EXAMPLE: The <u>man</u> with the brown dog <u>is going</u> home now.

1.   Our neighbor across the street is moving to Arizona.
2.   The lawyer's plea for mercy convinced the judge.
3.   The team wearing orange shirts came onto the field.

4.   The car in the other lane was crossing the center line.

5.   The car crossing the center line swerved just in time and did not hit us.

Check your answers on page 15 in the Answer Key for Book One. If you correctly identified the subject-verb combinations in 4 of 5 sentences, go to the Self-Check. If not, ask your instructor for help.

SELF-CHECK: SKILL UNIT 4

Below are two columns labeled <u>Subjects</u> and <u>Verbs or Verb Phrases</u>. Read the following sentences carefully. Write down all the subject-verb combinations in the sentences. If a subject or verb is compound, include the connecting word in your answer. If a subject is understood, write (you). Remember that a sentence can have several subject-verb combinations.

	Subjects	Verbs or Verb Phrases
EXAMPLE:	Harry I	watched went
1.		
2.		
3.		
4.		
5.		
6.		
7.		
8.		

	Subjects	Verbs or Verb Phrases
9.		
10.		
11.		
12.		
13.		
14.		
15.		

EXAMPLE: Harry watched the baby while I went to the store.

1. Harry and I played with the baby.
2. After Jerry finished his homework, he went to a movie.
3. Either Rebecca or I will win the race.
4. Over his head a huge flag was waving.
5. The grass in our yard died, but the weeds are still growing.
6. Is Abe running in the 400-meter race?
7. The dog across the street barked and howled all night.
8. Pass me the salt, please.
9. The value of that painting has increased.
10. Alice and Suzie worked on the project and then relaxed.
11. I will buy the food, Fran will order the flowers, and Jim will bring the chairs.
12. There were five men, six women, and three children at the party.
13. The woman talking with Hank ordered a search of the building.
14. Thelma asked for help, but Mr. Wilson refused it.
15. Stop asking questions and listen!

Check your answers on page 16 in the Answer Key for Book One. If you answered 12 of 15 items correctly, you have shown that you have mastered these skills. If not, ask your instructor for help.

Skill Unit 5
IDENTIFYING LINKING VERBS

What Skills You Need to Begin: You need to be able to identify nouns (Skill Unit 1), pronouns (Skill Unit 2), action verbs (Skill Unit 3), and subject-verb combinations in sentences (Skill Unit 4).

What Skills You Will Learn: After completing this skill unit, you will be able to identify linking verbs by the functions they perform in sentences. You will be able to tell the difference between linking verbs and helping verbs. You will also be able to tell the difference between linking verbs and action verbs.

Why You Need These Skills: Remember Tarzan? He was a great guy, but his English wasn't very good. He said, "Me Tarzan. You Jane." Among other things, Tarzan needed to learn about linking verbs so that he could say, "I <u>am</u> Tarzan. You <u>are</u> Jane." In these sentences, <u>am</u> and <u>are</u> are called linking verbs. Linking verbs perform important functions in sentences. Learning to distinguish linking verbs from helping verbs and action verbs will help you avoid common usage problems.

How You Will Show What You Have Learned: You will take the Self-Check at the end of this unit on page 88. The Self-Check consists of 20 sentences. If you correctly label the verbs as linking verbs, helping verbs, or action verbs in 15 of 20 sentences, you will have shown that you have mastered these skills.

If you feel that you have already mastered these skills, turn to the end of the unit and complete the Self-Check on page 88.

Subskill 5A: Recognizing That a Linking Verb Can Link the Subject to a Word That Renames the Subject

When you complete this subskill, you will be able to recognize that a linking verb can connect the subject with another word that renames the subject.

In Skill Unit 3, you learned that the verb in a sentence can express action. You have learned to recognize and use action verbs and their helpers. You know that the words <u>am</u>, <u>are</u>, <u>is</u>, <u>was</u>, <u>were</u>, <u>be</u>, <u>being</u>, and <u>been</u> can be used as helpers. When they are used as helpers, they help main verbs express different tenses.

S   V
Bill is looking for a sales job.

In this sentence, <u>is</u> is used as a helper to the main verb, <u>looking</u>. <u>Is looking</u> is an action verb phrase.

The words <u>am</u>, <u>are</u>, <u>is</u>, <u>was</u>, <u>were</u>, <u>be</u>, <u>being</u>, and <u>been</u> can also be used in a different way. They can be used as linking verbs. **A linking verb is used to connect, or link, the subject of a sentence with another word that either renames or describes the subject.** A linking verb doesn't show any kind of action.

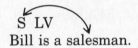
S LV
Bill is a salesman.

<u>Is</u> links the subject—Bill—to a phrase that renames Bill. In this sentence, <u>Bill</u> and <u>a salesman</u> are the same person. <u>Is</u> is used as a linking verb.

A linking verb acts as an equal sign. In math we can say:

2 + 2 = 4.

or we can say

2 + 2 is 4.

In the same way, the statement <u>Bill is a salesman</u> can be rewritten as <u>Bill = a salesman</u>. The linking verb <u>is</u> acts like an equal sign. It indicates that one noun or pronoun names the same person, place, or thing as another.

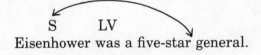
S   LV
Eisenhower was a five-star general.

The linking verb <u>was</u> indicates that in the past the word <u>general</u> and the word <u>Eisenhower</u> named the same person.

The verbs <u>is</u> and <u>was</u> are both forms of the verb <u>be</u>. We used <u>is</u> in our first example sentence to indicate a condition that exists in the present. We used <u>was</u> in our second example to indicate a condition that existed in the past.

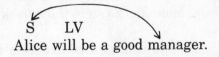
S   LV
Alice will be a good manager.

The linking verb phrase is <u>will be</u>. The main verb is <u>be</u>. The helper

<u>will</u> indicates future time. The noun <u>manager</u> renames Alice. The sentence tells us that in the future <u>Alice</u> and <u>manager</u> will name the same person.

Exercise for Subskill 5A

Read sentences A, B, and C. Answer the four questions about each sentence. Write your answers in the blanks.

A. Jim is a pilot.

    1. Which word in the sentence can be replaced by an equal sign? _____

    2. Which word in the sentence renames <u>Jim</u>? _____

    3. Which word is the linking verb? _____

    4. Does the linking verb show present, past, or future time? _____

B. The family is planning a picnic.

    5. Does the word <u>picnic</u> rename the family? _____

    6. Does the sentence contain an action verb or a linking verb? _____

    7. Can the words <u>is planning</u> be replaced by an equal sign? _____

    8. Is the word <u>is</u> being used as a helper? _____

C. Donna will be a teacher.

    9. Does the word <u>teacher</u> rename Donna? _____

    10. Does the sentence contain an action verb or a linking verb? _____

    11. Does the verb in the sentence show present, past, or future time? _____

    12. Does the sentence contain a helping verb? _____

    If so, write the helping verb here. _____

Check your answers on page 16 in the Answer Key for Book One. If you correctly answered 10 of 12 questions, go to Subskill 5B. If not, do the Supplemental Exercise for Subskill 5A.

Supplemental Exercise for Subskill 5A

A linking verb is a verb that connects, or links, the subject of a sentence with another word that either renames or describes the subject. The forms of the verb <u>be</u> (<u>am</u>, <u>is</u>, <u>are</u>, <u>was</u>, <u>were</u>, <u>be</u>, <u>being</u>, and <u>been</u>) are the most common linking verbs.

Read sentences A, B, and C. Answer the four questions about each sentence. Write your answers in the blanks.

A. Earl was a coach.

1. Which word in the sentence renames Earl? _____

2. Which word in the sentence can be replaced by an equal sign? _____

3. Which word is the linking verb? _____

4. Does the linking verb show present, past, or future time? _____

B. Ruth is buying a chair.

5. Does the word <u>chair</u> rename Ruth? _____

6. Does the sentence contain a linking verb? _____

7. Does <u>Ruth</u> equal a <u>chair</u>? _____

8. Is the verb phrase <u>is buying</u> an action verb phrase or a linking verb phrase? _____

C. Ruth will be an engineer.

9. Does the word <u>engineer</u> rename Ruth? _____

10. Does the verb in the sentence show present, past, or future time? _____

11. Which word in the sentence is a helping verb? _____

12. Is <u>will be</u> an action verb phrase or a linking verb phrase? _____

Check your answers on page 16 in the Answer Key for Book One. If you correctly answered 9 of 12 questions, go to Subskill 5B. If not, ask your instructor for help.

Subskill 5B: Recognizing That a Linking Verb Can Link the Subject to a Describing Word

When you complete this subskill, you will be able to recognize when a linking verb can connect the subject with a describing word.

Words that describe nouns or pronouns are called **adjectives.** You will study adjectives more fully in Skill Unit 6. Now, however, all you need to know is that linking verbs can connect the subject with a word that describes the subject.

S LV
Bill is happy.

The word <u>happy</u> describes Bill by telling what kind of person he is. The linking verb <u>is</u> connects the subject <u>Bill</u> with the describing word <u>happy</u>.

S   LV
My grandmother was kind.

The word <u>kind</u> describes grandmother by telling what kind of person she was. The linking verb <u>was</u> links the describing word <u>kind</u> with the subject <u>grandmother</u>.

Exercise for Subskill 5B

In the following sentences, underline the linking verb twice. Underline the subject once. Then draw an arrow from the subject to the word that describes it.

EXAMPLE: The <u>coat</u> <u>was</u> dirty.

1. Lee will be happy.

2. The tire was flat.

3. My paycheck is small.

4. The bus was late.

5. Ken has always been successful.

Check your answers on page 17 in the Answer Key for Book One. If you correctly answered all 5 items, go to Subskill 5C. If not, do the Supplemental Exercise for Subskill 5B.

Supplemental Exercise for Subskill 5B

A linking verb can connect a subject with a word that describes the subject.

S   LV
Consuela is funny.

In the above example, the linking verb is connects the subject <u>Consuela</u> with the word <u>funny</u>, which describes her.

In the following sentences, underline the linking verb twice. Underline the subject once. Then draw an arrow from the subject to the word that describes it.

EXAMPLE: The <u>test</u> <u>will be</u> hard.

1. The cat was white.

2. Kurt is always serious.

3. My new car will be heavier than my old one.

4. Our teacher was late.

5. Carol has been unhappy lately.

Check your answers on page 17 in the Answer Key for Book One. If you correctly answered all 5 items, go to Subskill 5C. If not, ask your instructor for help.

Subskill 5C: Identifying Linking Verbs Other Than <u>Be</u>

When you complete this subskill, you will be able to recognize when verbs other than <u>be</u> are used as linking verbs.

The verbs <u>seem</u> and <u>become</u> are almost always used as linking verbs.

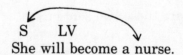
S   LV
She will become a nurse.

<u>Nurse</u> renames <u>she</u>. <u>Will become</u> links the subject <u>she</u> with a word that renames the subject.

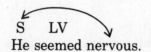
S   LV
He seemed nervous.

<u>Nervous</u> describes <u>he</u>. <u>Seemed</u> links the subject with a word that describes the subject.

Sometimes the verb <u>appear</u> has the same meaning as the verb <u>seem</u>. In that case, <u>appear</u> is a linking verb.

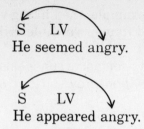

S   LV
He seemed angry.

S   LV
He appeared angry.

Sometimes, however, <u>appear</u> expresses action. In that case, it is an action verb.

S   V
Suddenly, the sun appeared on the horizon.

The verbs <u>feel</u>, <u>grow</u>, <u>smell</u>, <u>taste</u>, and <u>sound</u> can be either linking or action verbs, depending upon how they are used. If you can substitute a form of <u>seem</u> or <u>be</u> in a sentence so that the meaning is almost the same, the verb is functioning as a linking verb.

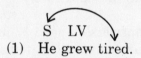

S   LV
(1)   He grew tired.

S   V
(2)   Betty grew vegetables.

In the first sentence, it is possible to substitute <u>was</u> or <u>seemed</u> for <u>grew</u>. You could say "He was tired" or "He seemed tired." In this sentence, the linking verb <u>grew</u> links the subject <u>he</u> with a word that describes the subject.

In the second sentence, there is no logical meaning if we say "Betty was vegetables" or "Betty seemed vegetables." In sentence 2, <u>grew</u> is an action verb that tells what Betty did.

Compare these two sentences:

S   LV
(1)   Mary felt sick.

S   V
(2)   Mary felt the damp wall.

You could say Mary <u>is</u> sick or Mary <u>seems</u> sick. The word <u>sick</u> describes the subject <u>Mary</u>. In sentence 1, <u>felt</u> is a linking verb that links the subject with a word that describes the subject.

You could not say "Mary is the damp wall." This does not make sense. In sentence 2, <u>felt</u> is an action verb that tells what Mary did. Apply what you have learned by doing the following exercise.

Exercise for Subskill 5C

Read sentences 1–10. If the verb in the sentence is used as a linking verb, write <u>LV</u> on the line after the sentence. If the verb expresses action, write <u>AV</u>.

EXAMPLE: The grapes tasted sour. <u>LV</u>

1. With more practice, Harry will become a better mechanic. ____
2. Betty grew tomatoes in pots. ____
3. Jim felt the back of his head. ____
4. Can you smell gas in this house? ____
5. Juan is becoming stronger every day. ____
6. The siren sounds terrible. ____
7. She feels lonely. ____
8. The warden sounded the alarm. ____
9. The solution to the problem seems simple. ____
10. That rose smells sweet. ____

Check your answers on page 17 in the Answer Key for Book One. If you correctly answered 8 of 10 items, go to the Self-Check. If not, do the Supplemental Exercise for Subskill 5C.

Supplemental Exercise for Subskill 5C

<u>Seem</u> and <u>become</u> are almost always used as linking verbs.

S   LV
Jean seemed content.

<u>Content</u> describes <u>Jean</u>. <u>Seemed</u> links the subject with a word that describes the subject.

<u>Appear</u>, <u>feel</u>, <u>grow</u>, <u>smell</u>, <u>taste</u>, and <u>sound</u> can be either linking verbs or action verbs, depending on how they are used. One way to tell whether one of these words is being used as a linking verb is to substitute a form of the verb <u>be</u> or <u>seem</u> in a sentence containing one of these words. If the meaning of the sentence is almost the same, then the word is being used as a linking verb.

Read sentences 1–10. If the verb in the sentence is used as a linking verb, write <u>LV</u> on the line after the sentence. If the verb expresses action, write <u>AV</u>.

EXAMPLE: Bert tasted the sour grapes.   <u>AV</u>

1.   Amy seemed angry.   ____

2.   The people in the waiting room are growing impatient.   ____

3.   Your idea sounds great.   ____

4.   I felt the fabric.   ____

5.   The fabric felt soft.   ____

6.   Tim is growing peppers and zucchini in his garden.   ____

7.   He smelled smoke.   ____

8.   This apple tastes good.   ____

9.   The cook tasted the soup.   ____

10.   That coffee smells wonderful.   ____

Check your answers on page 17 in the Answer Key for Book One. If you correctly answered 8 of 10 items, go to the Self-Check. If not, ask your instructor for help.

SELF-CHECK: SKILL UNIT 5

Part A.   In the sentences below, if the form of the verb <u>be</u> is being used as a helping verb, write <u>HV</u> on the line after the sentence. If the form of the verb <u>be</u> is being used as a linking verb, write <u>LV</u>.

EXAMPLE: After working all day, Angela <u>was</u> tired.   <u>LV</u>

1.   The men <u>are</u> coming to dinner tonight.   ____

2.   The men have not <u>been</u> very agreeable today.   ____

3.   The general <u>is</u> a good leader.   ____

4.   Carol will <u>be</u> waiting for you.   ____

5.   Charles has <u>been</u> a salesman for years.   ____

6.   I <u>am</u> going to the store.   ____

7.   <u>Am</u> I a good student?   ____

8.   <u>Was</u> Joe a big help around the house?   ____

9.   The students <u>were</u> still practicing at midnight.   ____

10.   Jane <u>was</u> sick all week.   ____

Part B. After each sentence, write LV if the underlined verb is a linking verb. Write AV if the verb is an action verb.

EXAMPLE: We <u>felt</u> sick after supper. <u>LV</u>

11. They seemed confused. _____

12. Larry <u>became</u> impatient with us. _____

13. That cheese <u>tasted</u> creamy. _____

14. Did he <u>become</u> a medical technician? _____

15. <u>Can</u> you <u>feel</u> your pulse? _____

16. <u>Do</u> you <u>feel</u> enthusiastic about the idea? _____

17. <u>Taste</u> this cheese. _____

18. I <u>am growing</u> tired of that program. _____

19. I <u>couldn't smell</u> anything. _____

20. That meatloaf <u>smells</u> good. _____

Check your answers on page 17 in the Answer Key for Book One. If you have correctly answered 15 of 20 items, you have shown that you have mastered these skills. If not, ask your instructor for help.

Skill Unit 6
IDENTIFYING ADJECTIVES

What Skills You Need to Begin: You need to be able to identify nouns (Skill Unit 1), pronouns (Skill Unit 2), linking verbs (Skill Unit 5), and subject–verb combinations in sentences (Skill Unit 4).

What Skills You Will Learn: When you complete this skill unit, you will be able to identify adjectives in sentences. You will be able to describe the use of adjectives as the answers to the questions "What kind?", "How much?", "How many?", and "Which one?" You will also recognize where adjectives can be placed in a sentence. You will be able to use adjectives to compare two or more nouns or pronouns, and you will identify and correct the error of using double forms of comparison.

Why You Need These Skills: An adjective modifies—or tells you something more about—nouns and pronouns. Suppose a friend were to tell you, "I met a man at a party." This wouldn't really tell you anything about the man. But what if your friend said, "I met a <u>drunk</u>, <u>annoying</u> man at the party," or, "I met an <u>interesting</u>, <u>handsome</u> man at the party." The words used to describe the noun <u>man</u> are adjectives. The different adjectives painted very different pictures of the man your friend met. The use of adjectives makes it possible to paint more interesting and more accurate pictures.

How You Will Show What You Have Learned: You will take the Self–Check at the end of this unit on page 98.. The Self-Check consists of 15 items. You will be asked to identify the adjectives in 10 sentences and choose between using <u>a</u> and <u>an</u> before a noun in 5 sentences. If you correctly complete 12 of 15 items, you will have shown that you have mastered these skills.

If you feel that you have already mastered these skills, turn to the end of this unit and complete the Self-Check on page 98.

Subskill 6A: Identifying the Use of Adjectives

When you complete this subskill, you will be able to identify adjectives. You will be able to describe adjectives as the answers to these questions about nouns and pronouns: "What kind?", "How much?", "How many?", or "Which one?" You will also be able to use <u>a</u> and <u>an</u> correctly in front of a noun.

What Is an Adjective?

An adjective is a word used to modify, or describe, nouns or pronouns. You remember from Skill Unit 1 that a noun names a person, place, or thing. And in Skill Unit 2, you learned that a pronoun stands in for a noun. When an adjective describes a noun or pronoun, it answers the question "What kind?", "How much?", "How many?", or "Which one?" Study the following sentences to see how an adjective describes a noun or a pronoun and makes the meaning clearer and more exact. (Throughout this Skill Unit, adjectives are underlined, nouns are marked <u>N</u>, and pronouns are marked <u>Pro</u>.)

N   N

The man drank the water.

N   N

The <u>thirsty</u> man drank the <u>muddy</u> water.

The adjective <u>thirsty</u> describes the noun <u>man</u>, and the adjective <u>muddy</u> describes the noun <u>water</u>.

N   N

A bear chased the hunter.

N   N

An <u>angry</u> <u>brown</u> bear chased the <u>frightened</u> hunter.

The adjectives <u>angry</u> and <u>brown</u> describe the noun <u>bear</u>. The adjective <u>frightened</u> describes the noun <u>hunter</u>.

You will remember from Skill Unit 5 that a linking verb can connect the subject (which is a noun or pronoun) to a word that describes the subject. That describing word is an **adjective.**

N

John is <u>happy</u>.

Pro

He is <u>happy</u>.

In the first sentence, <u>happy</u> is an adjective describing the noun <u>John</u>. In the second sentence, <u>happy</u> is an adjective describing the pronoun <u>he</u>.

Here is one way to help you identify adjectives in sentences. Think about the questions you might ask to get someone to give you a better description of someone, some place, or something.

Adjectives Can Answer the Question "What Kind?"

<pre>
         N   N
The <u>thirsty</u> man drank the <u>muddy</u> water.
</pre>

What kind of man? <u>thirsty</u>
What kind of water? <u>muddy</u>

Adjectives Can Answer the Questions "How Much" or "How Many?"

<pre>
                    N
Sam needed <u>more</u> time to do his work.
</pre>

How much time? <u>more</u>

<pre>
             N
I did <u>some</u> housework last night.
</pre>

How much housework? <u>some</u>

<pre>
               N   N
Bob had <u>four</u> interviews in <u>two</u> days.
</pre>

How many interviews? <u>four</u>
How many days? <u>two</u>

<pre>
   N
<u>Several</u> people left the show early.
</pre>

How many people? <u>several</u>

Adjectives Can Answer the Question "Which One?"

Remember from your study of pronouns that the words <u>this</u>, <u>that</u>, <u>these</u>, and <u>those</u> point out things or people. When these words are placed directly before nouns, they do the job of adjectives by answering the question "Which one?" Compare these two sentences:

    (1) <u>That</u> is my hat.

    (2) <u>That</u> hat is mine.

In sentence 1, <u>that</u> is used as a pronoun to point out. <u>That</u> is the subject of the sentence. In sentence 2, <u>that</u> is an adjective. It answers the question "Which hat?"

Using <u>A</u>, <u>An</u>, and <u>The</u> as Adjectives

In Skill Unit 1, you used the words <u>a</u>, <u>an</u>, and <u>the</u> to identify nouns. These three words are called **articles.** They do the job of adjectives by answering the question "Which one?" about nouns. In the exercises in this Skill Unit, you won't be asked to mark these words when you are asked to find adjectives. The only time these words cause problems is when you must decide whether to use a or an. Here are the rules to remember when choosing between a and an.

Rule 1:   Use an before words beginning with a vowel sound (a, e, i, o, u). Use this rule for words that begin with a silent h.

Rule 2:   Use a before words beginning with all other letters (consonants) and when the u at the beginning of a word sounds like you.

Vowel Sounds	**Consonant Sounds**
an apple	a sentence
an hour (the h is silent)	a hobby (the h is pronounced)
an umpire	a use (the u sounds like you)

Exercise for Subskill 6A

Part A.   Read sentences 1–5. Fill in each blank with an adjective from the following list. These adjectives should describe the nouns, marked with N. Do the exercise so that you use each adjective only once.

Adjectives

good	short
new	thin
cold	Four
several	That
~~fierce~~	~~tiny~~

           N   N

EXAMPLE: The fierce eagle caught a tiny mouse.

                 N   N

1. _____ restaurant served very _____ food.

                 N   N

2. The _____ wind blew down _____ trees.

                           N

3. I bought a _____ screwdriver.

                         N

4. The _____, _____ boy walked slowly down the street.

          N

5. _____ men were captured by the police.

Part B. Read sentences 6–10. In the spaces provided, write the question answered by each underlined adjective. You should write either "What kind?", "How many?", "How much?", or "Which one?"

EXAMPLE: It is going to be a <u>clear</u> day.   _____What kind?_____

6.   <u>That</u> student is quiet.   _____

7.   He has a <u>slight</u> scratch on his hand.   _____

8.   I need a <u>few</u> baseballs.   _____

9.   It is <u>thirteen</u> miles to my house.   _____

10.   Do you have <u>some</u> news for me?   _____

Part C. Read sentences 11–15. Show whether you would use <u>a</u> or <u>an</u> by circling the correct word.

EXAMPLE: He left (a, (an)) address where he could be reached.

11.   It should only take (a, an) hour to finish this.

12.   (A, An) child was looking for his mother.

13.   He had (a, an) hard time adjusting to civilian life.

14.   The workers wanted to start (a, an) union.

15.   Take (a, an) umbrella with you to work today.

Check your answers on pages 17 and 18 in the Answer Key for Book One. If you correctly answered all 15 questions, go to Subskill 6B. If not, do the Supplemental Exercise for Subskill 6A.

Supplemental Exercise for Subskill 6A

Adjectives are words that describe nouns or pronouns. They answer the questions "What kind?", "How much?", "How many?", or "Which one?" about a noun or pronoun. NOTE: The words <u>this</u>, <u>that</u>, <u>those</u>, and <u>these</u> are pronouns when they stand alone. They do the job of an adjective when they come in front of a noun and tell "which one."

Part A. Read sentences 1–6. In the space provided, write all the adjectives found in each sentence. Beside each adjective, write what question the adjective answers: "What kind?", "How much?", "How many?", or "Which one?" Review your work to make sure that you have completed each step.

EXAMPLE: This is a windy day.

   _____windy—What kind?_____

1.   That man fed the starving dog.

   _____

2. That is my best dress.

_____

3. Give me two copies of these reports.

_____

4. The frightened deer ran out of the burning forest.

_____

5. Two customers asked for more bread with their meal.

_____

6. The boys did not have much money to spend.

_____

Part B.   Read sentences 7–10. Show whether you would use _a_ or _an_ by circling the correct word.

EXAMPLE: Do you want to get ((a), an) pizza?

7. I would rather have (a, an) hamburger.
8. I had (a, an) argument with my brother Tom.
9. Does your new job require you to wear (a, an) uniform?
10. Anyone can make (a, an) honest mistake.

Check your answers on page 18 in the Answer Key for Book One. If you correctly answered 8 of 10 items, go to Subskill 6B. If not, ask your instructor for help.

Subskill 6B: Identifying the Placement of Adjectives

When you complete this subskill, you will be able to identify adjectives whether they are placed before or after the noun they describe.

Adjectives Can Be Placed Just Before a Noun

Most adjectives are placed before the nouns they describe. Look at the placement of the adjectives in these sentences.

N   N
The little child was frightened by the dark forest.

N
Twelve angry men were on the jury.

Adjectives Can Be Placed Just After a Noun

Adjectives can be placed after the nouns they describe. Sometimes this is done to add emphasis.

>   N
> The forest, <u>dark</u> and <u>gloomy</u>, frightened the child.

>   N
> The summer, <u>hot</u> and <u>dry</u>, seemed never to end.

Adjectives Can Be Placed After Linking Verbs

In Skill Unit 5, you learned that words describing nouns and pronouns often follow linking verbs. Those describing words are **adjectives.**

>   N
> Karen is <u>pretty</u>.

The adjective <u>pretty</u> follows the linking verb <u>is</u> in this sentence, but it still describes the noun <u>Karen</u>.

Exercise for Subskill 6B

Find all the adjectives in the following sentences. Then, do the following:

- Underline the adjectives.
- Draw an arrow from each adjective to the noun or pronoun it modifies.
- In the spaces below the sentence, write each adjective, the noun or pronoun it modifies, and the question that it answers—"What kind?", "How much?", "How many?", or "Which one?"

Review your work to be sure you have completed each step.

EXAMPLE: The wind, <u>cold</u> and <u>strong</u>, blew leaves and trash across the lawn.

cold—wind—What kind?

strong—wind—What kind?

1. Some music at the concert was terrible.

_____

2. Those dogs barked for five hours during the night.

_____

3. That joke is funny.

_____

4. The moon, full and bright, shone in the dark sky.

_____

_____

5. Those two women are detectives.

_____

_____

Check your answers on page 18 in the Answer Key for Book One. If you correctly identified the adjectives, the nouns they modified, and the questions they answered in all 5 sentences, go to the Self-Check. If not, do the Supplemental Exercise for Subskill 6B.

Supplemental Exercise for Subskill 6B

Find all the adjectives in sentences 1–5. Them do the following:

- Underline the adjectives.
- Draw an arrow from each adjective to the noun or pronoun it modifies.
- In the spaces below the sentence, write each adjective, the noun or pronoun it modifies, and the question that it answers—"What kind?", "How much?", "How many?", or "Which one?"

Review your work to be sure you have completed each step.

EXAMPLE: The angry father scolded his three children.

angry—father—What kind?

three—children—How many?

1. The athlete, lean and muscular, stretched before he ran.

_____

_____

2. Those children are lost.

_____

3. The survivors were helpless and few.

_____

4.   The two kittens were chased by a dog into some water.

_____

_____

5.   This cake has delicious frosting.

_____

Check your answers on pages 18 and 19 in the Answer Key for Book One. If you correctly identified the adjectives, the nouns they modified, and the questions they answered in 4 of 5 sentences, go to the Self-Check. If not, ask your instructor for help.

SELF-CHECK: SKILL UNIT 6

Part A.   Find all the adjectives in sentences 1–10. Then do the following:

· Underline the adjectives.

· Draw an arrow from each adjective to the noun or pronoun it modifies.

· In the spaces below the sentence, write each adjective, the noun or pronoun it modifies, and the question that it answers—"What kind?", "How much?", "How many?", or "Which one?"

Review your work to be sure you have completed each step.

EXAMPLE: That woman looks mysterious.

   that—woman—Which one?

   mysterious—woman—What kind?

1.   Those apples are sour.

_____

2.   The tall, skinny boy won the third race.

_____

_____

3.   The water, green and slimy, looked horrible.

_____

_____

4.   Several children caused a dreadful accident.

_____

_____

5. Three men contributed some money to the fund.

    _____

    _____

6. Have you read this new book?

    _____

    _____

7. Chris is tall and blond.

    _____

    _____

8. A few runners did not finish the difficult race.

    _____

    _____

9. The movie, long and boring, put everyone to sleep.

    _____

    _____

10. They were unhappy in their old apartment.

    _____

    _____

Part B. Read sentences 11–15. Show whether you would use <u>a</u> or <u>an</u> by circling the correct word.

EXAMPLE: I bought (ⓐ, an) coat with the money I saved.

11. Is Virginia (a, an) honest person?

12. I need (a, an) hammer to fix this door.

13. Mark just finished (a, an) unit in this book.

14. We took (a, an) airplane to Toronto.

15. You look like you've seen (a, an) ghost!

Check your answers on page 19 in the Answer Key for Book One. If you have correctly completed 12 of 15 items, then you have shown that you have mastered these skills. If not, ask your instructor for help.

Skill Unit 7
IDENTIFYING ADVERBS

What Skills You Need to Begin: You need to be able to identify nouns (Skill Unit 1), pronouns (Skill Unit 2), action verbs (Skill Unit 3), and linking verbs (Skill Unit 5). You should be able to recognize subject-verb combinations in sentences (Skill Unit 4) and be able to recognize adjectives (Skill Unit 6).

What Skills You Will Learn: When you complete this skill unit, you will be able to identify adverbs in sentences. You will be able to describe the use of adverbs as the answers to the questions "Where?", "When?", "How?", and "To what extent?" You will be able to spell adverb forms correctly. You will also be able to determine where to place an adverb in a sentence.

Why You Need These Skills: Adverbs modify—or tell you something more about—action verbs, adjectives, and other adverbs. Like adjectives, adverbs make your language more exact. For example, the sentence "The children played" doesn't tell you much about the action of playing. The meaning of the sentence can be changed by adding different adverbs to describe the verb. "The children played quietly" is very different from "The children played noisily." The adverbs quietly and noisily paint very different pictures of how the children played.

Adverbs can also change the pictures you paint with adjectives. You probably wouldn't want to work for a boss who was "almost always mean." But you wouldn't mind if your boss was "hardly ever mean." The adverbs almost, always, hardly, and ever gave very different meanings to the adjective mean.

How You Will Show What You Have Learned: You will take the Self–Check at the end of this unit on page 115. The Self–Check consists of 10 items. If you correctly identify the adverbs in 8 of 10 items, you will have shown that you have mastered these skills.

If you feel that you have already mastered these skills, turn to the end of this unit and complete the Self–Check on page 115.

Subskill 7A: Identifying the Use of Adverbs to Describe Action Verbs

When you complete this subskill, you will be able to identify adverbs when they are used to describe verbs. You will be able to describe adverbs as the answers to these questions about verbs: "Where?", "When?", and "How?"

What Is an Adverb?

An adverb is a word used to modify—or describe—an action verb, an adjective, or another adverb. We'll study the use of adverbs to describe adjectives and other adverbs in Subskill 7D. In this subskill, we'll look only at adverbs describing action verbs. You'll remember from Skill Unit 3 that an action verb tells what the subject of a sentence does, has done, or will do. You also remember that the action verb can be physical (as for the verb ran) or mental (as for the verb believe).

When an adverb modifies an action verb, it answers the questions "Where?", "When?", or "How?" Study the following sentences to see how an adverb describes an action verb and how different adverbs give different meanings to the action. (Throughout this Skill Unit, adverbs are underlined and verbs are marked V.)

V V
He has gone <u>outside</u>.
V V
He has gone <u>inside</u>.

The adverbs <u>outside</u> and <u>inside</u> describe the action verb phrase <u>has gone</u>. The adverbs tell you "where" he has gone.

V V
We are going <u>soon</u>.
V V
We are going <u>later</u>.

The adverbs <u>soon</u> and <u>later</u> describe the action verb phrase <u>are going</u>. The adverbs tell you "when" we are going.

V
Marge works <u>slowly</u>.
V
Marge works <u>quickly</u>.

The adverbs <u>slowly</u> and <u>quickly</u> describe the action verb <u>works</u>. The adverbs tell you "how" Marge works.

Using the questions "Where?", "When?", or "How?" after an action verb can help you identify adverbs.

Adverbs Can Answer the Question "Where?"

$$\overset{\text{V}}{\text{We looked}} \underline{\text{everywhere}} \text{ for you.}$$

looked <u>where</u>?   everywhere

$$\text{The horse } \overset{\text{V}}{\text{ran}} \underline{\text{home}}.$$

ran <u>where</u>?   home

Adverbs Can Answer the Question "When?"

$$\overset{\text{V}}{\text{We looked}} \text{ for you } \underline{\text{yesterday}}.$$

looked <u>when</u>?   yesterday

$$\text{The horse } \underline{\text{already}} \overset{\text{V}}{\text{ran}}.$$

ran <u>when</u>?   already

Adverbs Can Answer the Question "How?"

$$\underline{\text{Frantically}}, \overset{\text{V}}{\text{we looked}} \text{ for you.}$$

looked <u>how</u>?   frantically

$$\text{The horse } \overset{\text{V}}{\text{ran}} \underline{\text{fast}}.$$

ran <u>how</u>?   fast

Notice that the adverb didn't always come right after the verb in the examples. It didn't matter. You still found the adverbs by using the three questions. Use these steps to find adverbs in sentences:

(1) Find the action verb.

(2) Ask the questions "Where?", "When?", and "How?" after the verb.

(3) Any words that answer the questions are adverbs modifying the action verb.

Now try the question test to find the adverbs in the following exercise.

Exercise for Subskill 7A

Underline the adverbs in the following sentences. Decide which of the following questions the adverbs answer: "Where?", "When?", or "How?" After each sentence, write the question that has been answered by the adverb.

EXAMPLE: The cards were shuffled <u>well</u>.   ___How?___

1.   Please begin immediately.   _____

2.   Sometimes, I enjoy swimming.   _____

3.   Occasionally, I write poems.   _____

4.   I walk slowly.   _____

5.   Is your assignment done correctly?   _____

6.   Our dog sleeps lightly.   _____

7.   Outside, the summer roses bloomed.   _____

8.   The package will be sent back.   _____

9.   Nina jogged there.   _____

10.   Mr. Wilcox thought hard about the new plan.   _____

Check your answers on page 19 in the Answer Key for Book One. If you correctly identified each adverb and the question it answered in all 10 sentences, go to Subskill 7B. If not, do the Supplemental Exercise for Subskill 7A.

Supplemental Exercise for Subskill 7A

An adverb modifies an action verb, an adjective, or another adverb. When an adverb modifies an action verb, it answers the question "Where?", "When?", or "How?" You can find an adverb that modifies an action verb in a sentence by following these steps:

(1)   Find the action verb.

(2)   Ask the questions "Where?", "When?", and "How?" after the verb.

(3)   Any word that answers these questions is an adverb modifying the action verb.

Remember, an adverb can appear anywhere in a sentence. As long as a word answers one of the three questions about the action verb, it is an adverb.

Underline the adverbs in the following sentences. Decide which of the following questions the adverbs answer: "Where?", "When?", or "How?" After each sentence, write the question that has been answered by the adverb.

EXAMPLE: <u>Yesterday</u>, Lucy bought a new chair.   ___When?___

1. He agreed completely. _____

2. Cynthia suddenly stopped the car. _____

3. I left my wallet inside. _____

4. Floyd stood nearby. _____

5. Carefully, she picked up the eggs. _____

6. Watch closely. _____

7. Will you go now? _____

8. Bert answered quickly. _____

9. I will soon follow. _____

10. They met Nancy here. _____

Check your answers on page 20 in the Answer Key for Book One. If you correctly identified each adverb and the question it answered in 8 of 10 sentences, go to Subskill 7B. If not, ask your instructor for help.

Subskill 7B: Spelling Adverbs Correctly

When you complete this subskill, you will be able to spell adverbs that are formed from adjectives.

You may notice that many of the adverbs you see in this unit end with the letters <u>ly</u>. In most cases, you add <u>ly</u> to an adjective to make it an adverb.

ADJECTIVES:	frequent	successful	beautiful	nice
ADVERBS:	frequent<u>ly</u>	successful<u>ly</u>	beautiful<u>ly</u>	nice<u>ly</u>

EXAMPLES: My, what a beautiful baby.
(adjective describing the noun <u>baby</u>)

He smiles so beautiful<u>ly</u>.
(adverb describing the action verb <u>smiles</u>)

If the adjective ends with the letter y, you must change the y to i before adding ly.

ADJECTIVES: happy   hungry   ordinary
ADVERBS: happily   hungrily   ordinarily

EXAMPLES: Are you a hungry cat?
(adjective describing the noun cat)

He ate his food hungrily.
(adverb describing the action verb ate)

If the adjective ends with able or ible, you drop the e and add y to form the adverb.

ADJECTIVES: agreeable favorable horrible terrible
ADVERBS: agreeably favorably horribly terribly

EXAMPLES: I can't eat this terrible food.
(adjective describing the noun food)

You behaved terribly.
(adverb describing the action verb behaved)

Adding ly to an adjective is not always the correct way to form the adverb. Some adjectives do not change form when they become adverbs. The following words can serve as either adjectives or adverbs, depending on their use in a sentence:

daily	early
weekly	fast
monthly	hard
yearly	late

EXAMPLES: That was hard work.
(adjective describing the noun work)

I know you worked hard.
(adverb describing the action verb worked)

In the second example, you might have thought to yourself that the adverb hardly does exist. But it has a very different meaning from the adverb hard, as you can see in this example:

I know you hardly worked.

As shown in the list, the adjectives daily, weekly, monthly, yearly, and early can be used as adverbs. But not all adjectives that end with the letters ly can be used as adverbs. Study the examples on the following page:

YOU CAN SAY: I want my <u>weekly</u> paycheck.
(adjective describing the noun <u>paycheck</u>)

YOU CAN SAY: We are paid <u>weekly</u>.
(adverb describing the action verb phrase
<u>are paid</u>)

YOU CAN SAY: Sue is a <u>lovely</u> person.
(adjective describing the noun <u>person</u>)

YOU CANNOT SAY: She sings lovely.
(<u>lovely</u> cannot be used as an adverb to
describe the action verb <u>sings</u>)

Other adjectives that cannot become adverbs are: <u>friendly</u>, <u>lonely</u>, and <u>kindly</u>.

There are also a few adverbs that do not come from adjectives. These include the negative adverbs <u>not</u> and <u>never</u>, the adverbs <u>almost</u> and <u>ever</u>, and most of the adverbs that answer the question "Where?" or "When?" None of these adverbs may end with the letters <u>ly</u>. But you will know that they are adverbs by the work they do in describing action verbs.

Check your skill at identifying and spelling adverbs in the following exercise.

Exercise for Subskill 7B

Part A.   Read sentences 1–5. In each sentence, underline the adverb. If there is no adverb, write <u>NA</u> after the sentence.

EXAMPLE: The bird flew <u>high</u>. _____

1. Mr. Gentry was a lonely man. _____

2. Does she ever study? _____

3. Benita will leave early. _____

4. I am taking the early train. _____

5. Those are lovely flowers. _____

Part B.   Write the adverbs that are formed from the following adjectives.

	Adjectives	Adverbs
EXAMPLE:	merry	merrily
6.	possible	
7.	fast	

	Adjectives	Adverbs
8.	free	
9.	agreeable	
10.	dutiful	
11.	slow	
12.	warm	
13.	crazy	
14.	careful	
15.	rude	

Check your answers on page 20 in the Answer Key for Book One. If you correctly answered all 15 items, go to Subskill 7C. If not, do the Supplemental Exercise for Subskill 7B.

Supplemental Exercise for Subskill 7B

Review the spelling rules for changing adjectives to adverbs on pages 104–106. Then, do the following exercise.

Part A. Read sentences 1–5. In each sentence, underline the adverb. If there is no adverb, write <u>NA</u> after the sentence.

EXAMPLE: That is a hard problem.   <u>NA</u>

1. I worked hard on that problem. _____

2. Your dog is friendly. _____

3. I have never been to Europe. _____

4. Tom looked everywhere for his coat. _____

5. She is a fast runner. _____

Part B. Write the adverbs formed from the adjectives in items 6–15.

	Adjectives	Adverbs
EXAMPLE:	probable	probably
6.	early	
7.	easy	
8.	glad	

	Adjectives	Adverbs
9.	hopeful	
10.	complete	
11.	sensible	
12.	funny	
13.	hard	
14.	sharp	
15.	greedy	

Check your answers on pages 20 and 21. If you correctly answered 12 of 15 items, go to Subskill 7C. If not, ask your instructor for help.

Subskill 7C: Identifying the Placement of Adverbs

When you complete this subskill, you will be able to identify where adverbs can be placed in a sentence. You will be able to identify and correct adverb placement that makes the meaning of a sentence unclear.

Adverbs that modify action verbs can often be put in different places in sentences. Look at these sentences to see how many different places you can put the adverb slowly without changing the meaning:

Slowly, he walked down the street.

He slowly walked down the street.

He walked slowly down the street.

He walked down the street slowly.

No matter where you put it, the adverb still answers the same question about the same verb. You can use the question test you learned in Subskill 7A.

walked how?   slowly

A different kind of placement problem can happen with the adverbs only, just, and almost. Study the following examples to see how different placement of these adverbs can change the meaning completely.

(1)   I only cut my finger.

(2)   I cut only my finger.

(3) You <u>just</u> thought you could do it.

(4) You thought <u>just</u> you could do it.

(5) I <u>almost</u> bought a quart of ice cream.

(6) I bought <u>almost</u> a quart of ice cream.

In sentence 1, the adverb <u>only</u> modifies the verb <u>cut</u>. It's only a cut, not a deep wound. In sentence 2, the word <u>only</u> refers to the person's finger. The person didn't cut anything else.

In sentence 3, the adverb <u>just</u> modifies the verb <u>thought</u>. It was only a thought; the person couldn't really do it. In sentence 4, the word <u>just</u> gives the meaning "just you and nobody else."

In sentence 5, the adverb <u>almost</u> modifies the verb <u>bought</u>. The person did not buy ice cream. In sentence 6, the word <u>almost</u> refers to the ice cream. The person did buy ice cream, but it wasn't a full quart.

When you use adverbs, double-check to see that they clearly describe the words you want them to describe.

Exercise for Subskill 7C

In each of the following pairs of sentences, a word is shown in two different positions. Put an X in the blank after each sentence in which the word acts as an an adverb that modifies the underlined word. Remember, some adverbs can appear in different positions and still modify the verb. You may need to put an X in both blanks.

EXAMPLE: The bride and her father <u>walked</u> nervously down the aisle.
   <u>X</u>

The bride and her father <u>walked</u> down the aisle nervously.
   <u>X</u>

1. Eagerly, the crowd <u>waited</u> for the star to appear. _____

The crowd <u>waited</u> eagerly for the star to appear. _____

2. I just <u>saw</u> that new movie. _____

I <u>saw</u> just that new movie. _____

3. Often, people <u>get</u> sore throats in winter. _____

People often <u>get</u> sore throats in winter. _____

4. Only he <u>sprained</u> his thumb. _____

He only <u>sprained</u> his thumb. _____

5. We almost <u>moved</u> to Montreal. _____

We <u>moved</u> almost to Montreal. _____

Check your answers on page 21 in the Answer Key for Book One. If you correctly answered all 5 items, go to Subskill 7D. If not, do the Supplemental Exercise for Subskill 7C.

Supplemental Exercise for Subskill 7C

Review the rules and examples for correctly placing adverbs in sentences on pages 108 and 109. Then, do the following exercise.

In each of the following pairs of sentences, a word is shown in two different positions. Put an X in the blank after each sentence in which the word acts as an adverb that modifies the underlined word. Remember, some adverbs can appear in different positions and still modify the verb. You may need to put an X in both blanks.

EXAMPLE: Quickly, she <u>walked</u> down the street. _X_

She <u>walked</u> quickly down the street. _X_

1.   I sometimes <u>grow</u> tomatoes. ____

I <u>grow</u> tomatoes sometimes. ____

2.   He almost <u>left</u> a dollar on the table. ____

He <u>left</u> almost a dollar on the table. ____

3.   Immediately, the fire department <u>responded</u> to the alarm. ____

The fire department <u>responded</u> to the alarm immediately. ____

4.   Ms. Wu just <u>left</u> for the day. ____

Ms. Wu <u>left</u> just for the day. ____

5.   Sarah will soon <u>finish</u> the project. ____

Sarah will <u>finish</u> the project soon. ____

Check your answers on page 21 in the Answer Key for Book One. If you correctly answered 4 of 5 items, go to Subskill 7D. If not, ask your instructor for help.

Subskill 7D: Identifying the Use of Adverbs to Describe Adjectives and Adverbs

When you complete this subskill, you will be able to identify adverbs that modify adjectives and other adverbs.

Identifying Adverbs That Describe Adjectives

Just as adverbs can modify action verbs, they can also modify or add to the meaning of adjectives and other adverbs. When adverbs modify other adverbs or adjectives, they often answer the questions "To what extent?" or "How much?" Compare the following sentences. (Nouns are marked N, adjectives are marked Adj, and adverbs are marked Adv.)

Adj   N
Sally is a beautiful woman.

Here, beautiful describes the noun woman and answers the question "What kind?" Therefore, beautiful is an adjective.

Adv Adj   N
Sally is a very beautiful woman.

Here, very answers the question "How beautiful?"; that is, "To what extent" is Sally beautiful? It tells "how much" beauty Sally has. Therefore, very is an adverb that modifies the adjective beautiful.

Adj N
Ralph and Judy had a good time.

"What kind" of time did Ralph and Judy have? A good time. Here, good is an adjective that describes the noun time.

Adv Adj N
Ralph and Judy had a really good time.

Really answers the question "To what extent" did Ralph and Judy have a good time? It shows "how much" of a good time Ralph and Judy had. They had a really good time. Here really is an adverb because it modifies the adjective good. Really answers the question "How much?" about the adjective good. Notice that you must use the adverb really— not the adjective real—to describe an adjective.

By using different adverbs to describe an adjective, you can give different meanings to the adjective:

N   Adj
Linda is fairly shy.

N   Adj
Frank is extremely shy.

N   Adj
Mark is never shy.

All three sentences use the adjective shy after a linking verb to describe the subject nouns Linda, Frank, and Mark. Without the adverbs fairly and extremely, you wouldn't know "to what extent" Linda and Frank were shy. The adverbs let you know that Linda is not as shy as Frank. And the adverb never lets you know that Mark is not shy at all.

When you write, you may find that an adjective alone doesn't say exactly what you mean. This was true of the example sentences about Linda, Frank, and Mark. You can use an adverb in front of the adjective to describe "to what extent" the adjective describes the noun.

Identifying Adverbs That Describe Other Adverbs

You have seen how adverbs are used to describe both action verbs and adjectives. Study the following sentences to see how you can use adverbs to add to the meaning of other adverbs.

<blockquote>

                    V

(1) a. The choir sang softly.

               V   Adv

(1) b. The choir sang very softly.
</blockquote>

In sentence 1a, the adverb softly describes the action verb sang. It tells "how" the choir sang. In sentence 1b, the adverb very describes the adverb softly. It tells "how softly" the choir sang.

<blockquote>

                V

(2) a. Todd looked everywhere for his keys.

            V   Adv

(2) b. Todd looked almost everywhere for his keys.
</blockquote>

The word everywhere is an adverb. It answers the question "Where?" about the action verb looked. "Where" did Todd look? He looked everywhere. In sentence 2b, the meaning of the adverb everywhere is modified by adding the adverb almost. There is a difference between looking everywhere and almost everywhere for something that has been lost. Almost is an adverb modifying the adverb everywhere.

Placement of Adverbs That Describe Adjectives and Other Adverbs

In Subskill 7A, you identified and used adverbs that describe action verbs. In Subskill 7C, you learned that you could often put the adverb in several different places. This is not true for adverbs that describe adjectives and other adverbs. These adverbs are always placed just before the words they describe.

<blockquote>

                     Adv   Adj   N

Frank carried the extremely heavy package.
</blockquote>

Here the adjective heavy tells "what kind" about the noun package. The adverb extremely describes the adjective heavy. It tells "how heavy" the package was. The adverb extremely comes just before the adjective it describes.

        V   Adv Adv
     The car went very fast.

The adverb <u>fast</u> describes the action verb <u>went</u>. The adverb <u>very</u> comes just before the adverb <u>fast</u> and tells "how fast." It answers the question: "To what extent was the car going fast?"

Exercise for Subskill 7D

Read sentences 1–10 and find all the adverbs. Then, do the following:

- In the first column of the chart, write the adverbs.
- In the second column, write the words that the adverbs describe.
- In the third column, write what kind of word is being described by the adverb: verb, adjective, or adverb.

Review your work to be sure you have completed each step.

	Adverbs	Words Being Described	Kind of Word Being Described
EXAMPLE:	later much	will see later	verb adverb
1.			
2.			
3.			
4.			
5.			
6.			
7.			
8.			
9.			
10.			

EXAMPLE: I will see you much later.

1. My boss is unusually considerate.
2. Esther sews too slowly.
3. There was a rather large audience in the theater.
4. Paul just baked a pie.
5. Speak more distinctly!
6. This cake is very good.
7. Were there very many people at the wedding?
8. Have you ever seen that man?
9. Doris is never alone.
10. Linda is almost always tired.

Check your answers on page 22 in the Answer Key for Book One. If you correctly identified the adverbs and the words they described in all 10 sentences, go to the Self-Check. If not, do the Supplemental Exercise for Subskill 7D.

Supplemental Exercise for Subskill 7D

You know from your study of this unit that adverbs modify—or add to the meaning of—action verbs, adjectives, and other adverbs. Adverbs answer questions about the action verbs they modify. They also answer questions about the adjectives and adverbs they modify. Adverbs usually answer "How much?" or "To what extent?" about the adjectives and other adverbs they modify. Adverbs usually follow the action verbs they modify, but their position in the sentence can change. But adverbs that modify adjectives and other adverbs are always placed just before the words they modify.

Use the question test to help you complete the following chart.

Read sentences 1–10 on page 115 and find all the adverbs. Then do the following:

  · In the first column of the chart, write the adverbs.

  · In the second column, write the words that the adverbs describe.

  · In the third column, write what kind of word is being described by the adverb: verb, adjective, or adverb.

Review your work to be sure you have completed each step.

	Adverbs	Words Being Described	Kind of Word Being Described
EXAMPLE:	extremely hard	hard hits	adverb verb
1.			
2.			
3.			

	Adverbs	Words Being Described	Kind of Word Being Described
4.			
5.			
6.			
7.			
8.			
9.			
10.			

EXAMPLE: Peter hits extremely hard.

1. That is a very narrow bridge.
2. Listen very carefully!
3. Joe almost never hears what I say.
4. Her speech was too short.
5. The review was not favorable.
6. You play the guitar quite beautifully.
7. Luis is seldom late for work.
8. Angela buys the newspaper daily.
9. Sandra is always friendly to me.
10. They awoke early on Sunday.

Check your answers on page 22 in the Answer Key for Book One. If you correctly identified the adverbs and the words they described in 8 of 10 sentences, go to the Self-Check. If not, ask your instructor for help.

SELF-CHECK: SKILL UNIT 7

Find all the adverbs in sentences 1–10 on pages 116 and 117. Then, do the following:

- Underline the adverbs.

- Draw an arrow from each adverb to the verb, adjective, or adverb it modifies.

- In the spaces below the sentence, write each adverb. Then write the verb, adjective, or adverb it modifies, and the question it answers—"When?", "Where?", "How?", or "To what extent?"

Review your work to be sure you have completed each step.

EXAMPLE: We will go <u>home</u> <u>soon</u>.

         home—will go—Where?

         soon—will go—When?

1. Leave your umbrella and raincoat there.

2. Luisa almost never cries.

3. The ladder was rather shaky.

4. Occasionally, I eat lunch outside.

5. Beth is scarcely ever late.

6. The lonely boy walked slowly.

_____

_____

7. They quickly left the house but returned immediately.

_____

_____

8. Those children are not very happy.

_____

_____

9. I certainly never asked for that book.

_____

_____

10. Is Bernie very tired or just shy?

_____

_____

Check your answers on page 23 in the Answer Key for Book One. If you correctly answered 8 of 10 items, you have shown that you have mastered these skills. If not, ask your instructor for help.

Skill Unit 8
IDENTIFYING PREPOSITIONS
AND CONJUNCTIONS

What Skills You Need to Begin: You need to be able to identify nouns (Skill Unit 1), pronouns (Skill Unit 2), and verbs (Skill Units 3 and 5). You should also be able to identify subject-verb combinations (Skill Unit 4), adjectives (Skill Unit 6), and adverbs (Skill Unit 7).

What Skills You Will Learn: When you complete this skill unit, you will be able to identify prepositions and conjunctions and describe the work they do in sentences.

Why You Need These Skills: You have learned to identify nouns, pronouns, verbs, adverbs, and adjectives in sentences. There are just two other kinds of words used in sentences—prepositions and conjunctions. These two kinds of words help you make connections between the other kinds of words you have studied. Look at this example:

WITHOUT PREPOSITIONS
OR CONJUNCTIONS: The barn was burning. The horse was frightened. The fire frightened him. He kicked his stall. He ran outside. He was safe.

WITH PREPOSITIONS
AND CONJUNCTIONS: The horse was frightened <u>by the fire</u> <u>in the burning barn</u>. He kicked his stall <u><u>and</u></u> ran outside <u>to safety</u>.

    The prepositional phrases are underlined once, and the conjunction is underlined twice. The prepositions and the conjunction allow us to get all the information in two sentences rather than six. Also, the connections between the ideas are stronger when prepositions and conjunctions are used.

How You Will Show What You Have Learned: You will take the Self–Check at the end of this unit on page 127. The Self-Check consists of 10 sentences. If you correctly identify the prepositions, the objects of the prepositions, the conjunctions, and the words or phrases connected by the conjunctions in 8 of 10 sentences, you will have shown that you have mastered these skills.

If you feel that you have already mastered these skills, turn to the end of this unit and complete the Self–Check on page 127.

Subskill 8A: Identifying the Use of Prepositions

When you complete this subskill, you will be able to identify prepositions, prepositional phrases, and objects of prepositions. You will be able to describe how prepositional phrases do the work of adjectives or adverbs.

A **preposition** is a kind of linking word. It shows how a noun or pronoun is related to a verb or to another noun or pronoun. The prepositions in these sentences are underlined.

Your purse is <u>in</u> the suitcase.

Your purse is <u>beside</u> the suitcase.

Your purse is <u>on</u> the suitcase.

Your purse is <u>near</u> the suitcase.

Your purse is <u>under</u> the suitcase.

In each of the above sentences, the prepositions link the noun <u>suitcase</u> with the noun <u>purse</u> by telling where the purse is in relation to the suitcase.

She will not leave <u>before</u> Monday.

She will not leave <u>after</u> Monday.

She will not leave <u>until</u> Monday.

The prepositions in the above examples link the noun <u>Monday</u> with the verb <u>will leave</u> by telling when <u>she</u> will leave in relation to Monday.

There are many prepositions. The chart on the following page lists fifty prepositions you probably use all the time. Study the chart and the examples after the chart to see how many different kinds of relationships prepositions can show.

Prepositions		
about	beyond	on
above	but (meaning	out
across	"except")	outside
after	by	over
against	concerning	past
along	despite	since
amid	down	through
among	during	throughout
around	except	to
as	for	toward
at	from	under
before	in	until
behind	inside	up
below	into	upon
beneath	like	with
beside	of	within
between	off	without

EXAMPLES: light <u>above</u> my bed

the house <u>across</u> the street

place <u>after</u> the verb

work <u>at</u> the restaurant

finish <u>before</u> tomorrow

the space <u>between</u> our desks

leave <u>by</u> sundown

everyone <u>except</u> me

ticket <u>for</u> the show

gift <u>from</u> our boss

bird <u>in</u> the cage

dive <u>into</u> the water

end <u>of</u> the movie

sitting <u>on</u> the chair

jump <u>over</u> the fence

gone <u>since</u> yesterday

leap <u>through</u> the air

go <u>to</u> the store

going <u>toward</u> the east

swimming <u>under</u> water

wait <u>until</u> tomorrow

step <u>up</u> the ladder

boat <u>upon</u> the water

tea <u>with</u> honey

stay <u>within</u> the lines

The group of words that begins with a preposition is called a **prepositional phrase.** The noun or pronoun at the end of the phrase is called the **object of the preposition.** The prepositional phrases are underlined in the following examples:

My son is the child <u>with curly hair</u>.

Notice that in a prepositional phrase one or more words can come between the preposition and the object of the preposition. In the sentence above, the adjective <u>curly</u> comes between the preposition and the object noun. In this sentence, <u>with curly hair</u> is a prepositional phrase beginning with the preposition <u>with</u> and ending with the noun <u>hair</u>. The noun <u>hair</u> is the object of the preposition <u>with</u>.

You will recall from Skill Unit 6 that adjectives answer the questions "What kind?", "How much?", "How many?", and "Which one?" about nouns and pronouns. Prepositional phrases can also do the work of adjectives. When they do, they almost always answer the question "Which one?" To see how this works, look at these prepositional phrases:

the car <u>with the hatchback</u>
the house <u>around the corner</u>

The phrase <u>with the hatchback</u> describes the noun <u>car</u> and tells "which one." The phrase <u>around the corner</u> describes the noun <u>house</u> and tells "which one."

Some prepositional phrases do the work of adverbs. In Skill Unit 7, you learned that adverbs answer the questions "Where?", "When?", "How?", and "To what extent?" about verbs, adjectives, and other adverbs. Prepositional phrases may also answer these questions about verbs. Look at these prepositional phrases to see how this works:

The jogger ran <u>down the road</u>.   (Where?)

The jogger ran <u>before sunrise</u>.   (When?)

The jogger ran <u>with long strides</u>.   (How?)

The jogger ran <u>for a few minutes</u>.   (To what extent?)

All of these phrases describe the verb <u>ran</u>.

Exercise for Subskill 8A

Read sentences 1–10 and do the following:

- Underline the prepositions once.
- Underline the objects of the prepositions twice.
- Circle the prepositional phrases.

There may be more than one prepositional phrase in a sentence. Review your work to be sure you have completed each step.

EXAMPLE: Will you be going (to the <u>mall</u>) today?

1. Frank, put your clothes in the closet!

2. Grace looked longingly at the gold necklace in the jewelry case.

3.   Holidays are busy times for everyone.

4.   Hal and Marcia had dinner at Wendy's before the game.

5.   Is Zita going to the dance with Lonnie?

6.   Everyone went to Barry's house after the game.

7.   All of the plants in the greenhouse were frozen

during the blizzard.

8.   Mr. Franks, the shop instructor, bought a 2″ × 4″

at the lumber yard for the special project.

9.   Everyone in the aerobics class but Francie lost weight.

10. Megan forgot the sugar in the cookie batter.

Check your answers on pages 23 and 24 in the Answer Key for Book One. If you correctly identified the prepositional phrases in all 10 sentences, go to Subskill 8B. If not, do the Supplemental Exercise for Subskill 8A.

Supplemental Exercise for Subskill 8A

A preposition is a word that comes before a noun or pronoun. It shows how the noun or pronoun is related to a verb or to another noun or pronoun. Review the list of common prepositions on page 120.

A prepositional phrase is a group of words that begins with a preposition and acts as an adjective or adverb.

The object of the preposition is the noun or pronoun at the end of the prepositional phrase.

Read sentences 1–10 on page 123 and to the following:

- Underline the prepositions once.
- Underline the objects of the prepositions twice.
- Circle the prepositional phrases.

There may be more than one prepositional phrase in a sentence. Review your work to be sure you have completed each step.

EXAMPLE: The animals (in the zoo) are given special diets (by the veterinarians).

1. The race for chairperson was between John and me.

2. Eileen and Joe were among the guests at the wedding.

3. The cat knocked the pitcher off the counter and onto the floor.

4. Tim ran across the street with James.

5. Interest rates on mortgage loans decreased by 2%

   during November.

6. Many nervous applicants still present themselves well

   during job interviews.

7. As Herb drove toward Los Angeles, he realized that he

   was driving without his license.

8. The baby cried throughout the concert, but his parents still

   didn't take him from the auditorium.

9. Should I wait for them until sunset?

10. The band from Richland High marched very carefully

    behind the horses.

Check your answers on page 24 in the Answer Key for Book One. If you correctly identified the prepositional phrases in 8 of 10 sentences, go to Subskill 8B. If not, ask your instructor for help.

Subskill 8B: Identifying the Use of Conjunctions

When you complete this subskill, you will be able to identify conjunctions and describe the work they do in sentences.

In Subskill 4B, you learned that compound subjects and compound verbs are connected by the words <u>and</u>, <u>or</u>, or <u>nor</u>. These words are called conjunctions. **A conjunction is a word used to join two or more equal words, phrases, or statements.** In compound subjects and compound verbs, the conjunctions join words. Look at a few examples to refresh your memory. The conjunctions in the following examples have been underlined:

The men <u>and</u> women played Bingo at our church.

In this sentence, the conjunction <u>and</u> connects the two nouns <u>men</u> and <u>women</u>. The conjunction <u>and</u> tells you that both subjects performed the same action.

Were you working <u>or</u> sleeping?

In this sentence, the conjunction <u>or</u> connects the verbs <u>working</u> and <u>sleeping</u>. The conjunction <u>or</u> tells you that there is a choice of two possible actions the subject could be doing.

In both these sentences, the conjunctions connect two words that do the same job in each sentence. In the first sentence, the conjunction <u>and</u> joins two nouns used as subjects. In the second, the conjunction <u>or</u> connects two verbs.

There are only a few conjunctions for you to remember. They are <u>and</u>, <u>but</u>, <u>for</u>, <u>or</u>, <u>nor</u>, <u>yet</u>, and <u>so</u>. Look at some sentences in which these conjunctions are used.

NOUN TO NOUN: Jay <u>and</u> Ramon went to the movies.

NOUN TO PRONOUN: I'll give either Greg <u>or</u> you the ticket.

PRONOUN TO PRONOUN: Neither you <u>nor</u> I will ever know the truth.

VERB TO VERB: The fighter shook his head <u>and</u> slowly staggered to his corner.

ADJECTIVE TO ADJECTIVE: Arthur is smart <u>but</u> lazy.

ADVERB TO ADVERB: She spoke powerfully <u>yet</u> slowly.

PHRASE TO PHRASE: Should I take the job at the supermarket <u>or</u> at the warehouse?

STATEMENT TO STATEMENT: I want you to come with me, <u>for</u> Martin's car was out of gas, <u>so</u> he walked to the nearest station.

In the example sentences for nouns and pronouns, notice that the conjunction <u>or</u> is used with the word <u>either</u>. The conjunction <u>nor</u> is used with the word <u>neither</u>. These words are often paired. When you use these pairs, make sure you use <u>either</u> (never <u>neither</u>) with the conjunction <u>or</u>. Use <u>neither</u> with the conjunction <u>nor</u>.

Sometimes you will want to connect more than two words or phrases. The conjunction should be placed only in front of the last word in the series.

I've collected butterflies, stamps, model cars, <u>and</u> coins.

I don't feel healthy, wealthy, <u>or</u> wise.

Exercise for Subskill 8B

Read sentences 1–10 on pages 125 and 126 and do the following:

- First, circle all the conjunctions you find.

- Then, in the following chart, write down each conjunction and tell if the conjunction connects word to word, phrase to phrase, or statement to statement.

- If there is no conjunction, write an <u>X</u> in the space provided.

Review your work to be sure you have completed each step.

	The Conjunction Is	The Conjunction Connects
EXAMPLE:	and	word to word
1.		
2.		
3.		
4.		
5.		
6.		
7.		
8.		
9.		
10.		

EXAMPLE: My family (and) I learned a valuable lesson last Christmas.

1. Right before Christmas, my youngest son found a neighbor sitting on her front porch crying, so he asked if he could help.

2. She was upset and worried, for she was short on money.

3. She could not afford to buy Christmas presents or food for Christmas dinner.

4. We invited them to our house for dinner, and our kids offered to share their toys.

5. On Christmas Day, the woman and her family came to our house.

6. We had gifts for the children and for the parents.

7. We also had a big turkey, so everyone had plenty to eat.

8. After dinner, we played games and sang.

9. Our neighbor thanked us tearfully yet happily.

10. This must be the true meaning of Christmas.

Check your answers on pages 24 and 25 in the Answer Key for Book One. If you correctly identified the conjunctions and what they connect in all 10 sentences, go to the Self–Check. If not, do the Supplemental Exercise for Subskill 8B.

Supplemental Exercise for Subskill 8B

A conjunction is a word used to join two or more equal words, phrases, or statements. Conjunctions include the words and, but, for, or, nor, yet, and so. In the following examples, the conjunctions are underlined twice and the words, phrases, or statements they connect are underlined once.

WORD TO WORD: Diving and swimming are my favorite sports.

I either swim or run every day.

PHRASE TO PHRASE: Inez was so sick that she went neither to work nor to school.

STATEMENT TO STATEMENT: Alma loved Oscar, yet she was not happily married.

Now, try your hand at identifying the conjunctions in this passage.

Read sentences 1–6 on page 127 and do the following:

- First, circle all the conjunctions you find.
- Then, in the following chart, write down each conjunction and tell if the conjunction connects word to word, phrase to phrase, or statement to statement.
- If there is no conjunction, write an X in the space provided.

Review your work to be sure you have completed each step.

	The Conjunction Is	The Conjunction Connects
EXAMPLE:	yet	statement to statement
1.		
2.		
3.		
4.		
5.		
6.		

EXAMPLE: The dollar is worth less every year, (yet) you can try to make it go further with careful planning.

1. You need a budget based upon your income and upon your expenses.

2. Then you must stick to the budget throughout the month, so you will not spend more than you make.

3. A good habit is cutting coupons from newspapers or magazines, for coupons can help you save money when you shop.

4. You can also check grocery ads for special sales, but you shouldn't buy things you don't need just because they're on sale.

5. Don't forget to put aside money for regular payments on installment purchases or for unexpected emergencies.

6. You can try to beat inflation, but you have to be smart about shopping and about spending.

Check your answers on pages 25 and 26 in the Answer Key for Book One. If you correctly identified the conjunctions and what they connect in 4 of 6 sentences, go to the Self-Check. If not, ask your instructor for help.

SELF-CHECK: SKILL UNIT 8

Read sentences 1–10 on page 129. Then, do the following:

- Identify the prepositional phrases and write the prepositions in the first column of the following chart.
- Write the objects of the prepositions in the second column.
- Write the conjunctions you find in the third column.
- In the fourth column, write whether the conjunction connects word to word, phrase to phrase, or statement to statement.

Review your work to be sure you have completed each step.

	The Preposition Is	The Object of the Preposition Is	The Conjunction Is	The Conjunction Connects
EXAMPLE:	for	diet	so	statement to statement
1.				
2.				
3.				
4.				
5.				
6.				

	The Preposition Is	The Object of the Preposition Is	The Conjunction Is	The Conjunction Connects
7.				
8.				
9.				
10.				

EXAMPLE: I couldn't button my jacket today, so I know it's time for a diet.

1. I can buy some new clothes, or I can lose some weight.
2. I've had this problem for years, but I just can't lose weight.
3. I've tried every diet and every exercise program.
4. I've used hypnosis and fasting.
5. I've tried everything, yet I still weigh more than I would like.
6. I'm a big fan of Dr. Stillman and Dr. Atkins.
7. I know them well, yet I'm still searching for my diet guru.
8. I've starved myself on diets of bananas, grapefruits, raw vegetables, and water.
9. Unfortunately, these diets don't work, and I'm tired of them.
10. I think I'll just buy some new clothes.

Check your answers on page 26 in the Answer Key for Book One. If you correctly identified the prepositions, the objects of the prepositions, the conjunctions, and the words or phrases connected by the conjunctions in 8 of 10 sentences, you have shown that you have mastered these skills. If not, ask your instructor for help.

Skill Unit 9
IDENTIFYING SIMPLE SENTENCES

What Skills You Need to Begin: You need to be able to identify nouns (Skill Unit 1), pronouns (Skill Unit 2), and verbs (Skill Units 3 and 5). You should also be able to recognize subject-verb combinations (Skill Unit 4), adjectives (Skill Unit 6), adverbs (Skill Unit 7), and prepositions and conjunctions (Skill Unit 8).

What Skills You Will Learn: When you complete this skill unit, you will be able to identify the parts of a complete sentence. You will be able to identify the elements in the following sentence patterns: subject + action verb (S + V); subject + action verb + direct object (S + V + DO); subject + action verb + indirect object + direct object (S + V + IO + DO); and subject + linking verb + subject complement (S + LV + SC).

Why You Need These Skills: You are now armed with the basic kinds of words used to make sentences—nouns, pronouns, verbs, adjectives, adverbs, prepositions, and conjunctions. You already know many of the jobs these kinds of words do in sentences. For example, in Skill Unit 4, you learned to identify the two things every sentence must have—a subject and a verb. And from Skill Units 6, 7, and 8, you know that you can use adjectives, adverbs, and prepositional phrases to do the jobs of describing the nouns, pronouns, and verbs in a sentence.

In this unit, you'll learn about three other jobs words can do in a sentence. They can be direct objects, indirect objects, or subject complements. You need to be able to identify when a word is doing one of these three jobs because only certain kinds of words can do these jobs. Choosing the right word for the job is the key to building sentences according to the rules of standard English.

How You Will Show What You Have Learned: You will take the Self–Check at the end of this unit on page 158. You will be asked to identify subjects, verbs, indirect objects, direct objects, and subject complements in 15 sentences. If you correctly answer 12 of 15 items, you will have shown that you have mastered these skills.

If you feel that you have already mastered these skills, turn to the end of this unit and complete the Self–Check on page 158.

Subskill 9A: Identifying Subject + Action Verb Sentences

When you complete this subskill, you will be able to identify a subject + action verb sentence pattern. You will be able to identify when this kind of sentence is a complete sentence.

In Skill Unit 4, you learned to identify the subject and the verb of a sentence. A subject and a verb form the most basic sentence. In the following sentences, the subjects are marked S and the verbs are marked V.

$$\text{S} \quad \text{V}$$
Fred ran.

$$\text{S} \quad \text{V}$$
They understand.

Each sentence is made up of only two words. Yet each is a **complete sentence.** No other words are really needed to state a complete idea. The subject—which can be a noun or a pronoun—tells you who or what the sentence is about. And the verb tells you what the subject does.

To be complete, a sentence must tell who or what the sentence is about by supplying a subject. It must also tell something about the subject by supplying a verb.

Identifying Complete Sentences With More Than One Subject or Verb

There are several ways you can build on the subject and verb of a complete sentence. You can use conjunctions to make either a compound subject or a compound verb. You can also add adjectives to describe the subject and adverbs to describe the verb. In the examples in this unit, adjectives are marked Adj and adverbs are marked Adv.

Compound Subject

$$\text{S} \quad \text{V}$$
Henry will go.

$$\text{S} \qquad \text{S} \quad \text{V} \quad \text{Adv}$$
Henry and Frank will go tomorrow.

The first sentence has one subject—Henry—plus one action verb phrase—will go. The second sentence adds a second subject—Frank—with the conjunction and. We call two or more subjects that share the action of the verb a **compound subject.** The second sentence also adds the adverb tomorrow to answer the question "When?" about the verb phrase will go.

Compound Verb

> S   V
> Hester can sing.
>
> S   V   V
> Hester can sing and dance.

The subject of both sentences is the single noun Hester. The second sentence adds the verb dance to the verb phrase can sing with the conjunction and. We call two or more verbs joined together by conjunctions a **compound verb.**

Compound Subject and Compound Verb

> S V
> Lin ate.
>
> S   S   V   V   Adv
> Lin and Mei Ling ate and drank slowly.

In the first sentence, we have one subject plus one action verb. In the second sentence, we have a compound subject—Lin and Mei Ling— and a compound verb—ate and drank. The two subjects and the two verbs are connected by the conjunction and. The second sentence also adds the adverb slowly to answer the question "How?" about the verbs ate and drank.

Understood Subjects

You may remember from Skill Unit 4 that the subjects of commands and requests are usually not stated. We understand that the subject of these kinds of sentences is you. Thus, for these kinds of sentences, you may need only one word—the verb—to have a complete sentence. For example, "Stop!" is a complete sentence. The subject of the verb stop is understood to be you. But we can add to these one-word sentences by using conjunctions and adverbs.

> S   V
> (You) Stop!
>
> S   V   V   Adv
> (You) Stop and think now!

In the examples, we put the subject you in parentheses to show that it is not usually written as part of the sentence. In the second sentence, we have a compound verb—stop and think—joined with the conjunction and. And we added the adverb now to answer the question "When?" about the verbs stop and think.

Adding Prepositional Phrases to Subject + Action Verb Sentences

In Skill Unit 8, you learned to identify prepositional phrases in sentences. You also learned that the prepositional phrase can do the work of an adjective or an adverb. Look at the following examples to review how this works.

S   V

The man sang.

Adj S V

The loud man sang.

The first sentence has one subject plus one action verb. In the second sentence, we added the adjective <u>loud</u> to answer the question "What kind?" about the noun <u>man</u>. Now let's substitute a prepositional phrase for the adjective <u>loud</u>. (Prepositional phrases are marked <u>Prep Phrase</u>.)

Prep. Phrase

S ⌒ V

The man with the loud voice sang.

Here, the prepositional phrase <u>with the loud voice</u> answers the question "What kind?" The prepositional phrase is doing the work of an adjective.

You can add more than one prepositional phrase to a sentence.

Prep. Phrase Prep. Phrase

S ⌒ ⌒ V

The phone on the table in the bedroom is

Adv V

not working.

The prepositional phrases <u>on the table</u> and <u>in the bedroom</u> describe the noun <u>phone</u> and answer the question "Which one?"

Now, let's add an adverb to a sentence with a subject and an action verb.

S   V

Help will arrive.

S   V   Adv

Help will arrive soon.

In the second sentence, <u>soon</u> answers the question "When?" about the action verb phrase <u>will arrive</u>. Therefore, <u>soon</u> is an adverb. If we substitute a prepositional phrase, it too will answer the question "When?"

```
                           Prep. Phrase
        S      V          ⌒‿‿‿‿⌒
      Help will arrive in a minute.
```

The phrase <u>in a minute</u> is doing the work of an adverb.

As you can see in the following example, a subject + action verb sentence can become quite long simply by adding adjectives, adverbs, and prepositional phrases.

```
      S    V
    People run.

                         Prep. Phrase
      Adj      S        ⌒‿‿‿‿⌒      V
    The athletic people in my neighborhood run

        Prep. Phrase  Prep. Phrase
    Adv ⌒‿‿‿⌒  ⌒‿‿⌒
    early in the morning on weekends.
```

Identifying Complete Sentences When the Subject and Verb Are Inverted

In Skill Unit 4, you learned to identify the subject and verb in sentences in which the verb or part of the verb phrase comes before the subject. This happens when:

· the sentence is a question

· the sentence begins with <u>here</u> or <u>there</u>

Look at these examples:

```
      Adv  V      S     V
    Where are the children eating?

                           Prep. Phrase
      V      S     V      ⌒‿‿⌒
    Are the children eating with us?
```

In these examples, the subject–verb pattern is inverted because the examples are questions. The subject of both questions is the noun <u>children</u>. Both questions have the same action verb phrase—<u>are eating</u>. In the first question, we used the word <u>where</u>. Question words work much like adverbs. In the second question, we added the prepositional phrase <u>with us</u> to the basic subject + action verb pattern.

```
                              Prep. Phrase
      V  Adv Adj    S        ⌒‿‿⌒
    There were too many people on the train.
```

In this example, the subject–verb pattern is inverted because the sentence starts with the word <u>there</u>. An adverb, an adjective, and a prepositional phrase have been added to the basic subject + action verb pattern.

As you can see, the subject + action verb sentence pattern can have any of the following:

- a single subject

- a single verb

- a compound subject

- a compound verb

- a compound subject and a compound verb

- an understood subject

- an inverted subject-verb combination

- one or more adjectives or adverbs to describe the subject or the verb

- one or more prepositional phrases to describe the subject or the verb

Now, check your ability to identify the parts you need to make a complete sentence in the following exercise. All the sentences use a subject + action verb pattern.

Exercise for Subskill 9A

Read sentences 1–10 on page 136 and do the following:

- Write all subjects in the column labeled <u>Subjects</u>. If the subject is understood, write <u>you</u> in parentheses in this column.

- Write all verbs in the column labeled <u>Verbs</u>.

- If either the subjects or the verbs are compound, include the conjunctions.

Review your work to be sure you have completed each step.

	Subjects	**Verbs**
EXAMPLE:	child and mother	walked
1.		
2.		
3.		

	Subjects	Verbs
4.		
5.		
6.		
7.		
8.		
9.		
10.		

EXAMPLE: The child in the blue coat and his mother walked through the park.

1.   Philip and Josie bowed to the audience.
2.   The dictionary with the blue cover fell off the shelf.
3.   The ambulance should arrive in a few minutes.
4.   Run to the office and ask for help!
5.   Will we leave at noon?
6.   We waited inside the theater.
7.   Go to the store around the corner.
8.   Many students study at the last minute.
9.   Several children in the group raced to the end of the block.
10. He slept until noon.

Check your answers on page 27 in the Answer Key for Book One. If you correctly identified the subjects and verbs in all 10 sentences, go to Subskill 9B. If not, do the Supplemental Exercise for Subskill 9A.

Supplemental Exercise for Subskill 9A

A complete sentence must have a subject and a verb. A subject tells you who or what the sentence is about. A verb tells you something about the subject.

The simplest sentence pattern is the subject + action verb (S + V) pattern. The action verb tells you what the subject does, did, or will do. This pattern can contain a single or compound subject, a single or compound action verb, a compound subject and compound action verb, or an understood subject. This pattern may also be inverted in questions and in sentences that begin with here or there. You can also add adjectives, adverbs, and prepositional phrases to the basic pattern of subject + action verb.

Read sentences 1–10 and do the following:

- Write all subjects in the column labeled <u>Subjects</u>. If the subject is understood, write <u>you</u> in parentheses in this column.

- Write all verbs in the column labeled <u>Verbs</u>.

- If either the subjects or the verbs are compound, include the conjunctions.

Review your work to be sure you have completed each step.

	Subjects	Verbs
EXAMPLE:	screams	rang
1.		
2.		
3.		
4.		
5.		
6.		
7.		
8.		
9.		
10.		

EXAMPLE: The screams of terror rang through the theater.

1. Are you and he going to town?
2. Butler and Evan ran across the lawn and jumped in the pool.
3. Mary's bookbag fell into the mud.
4. The audience clapped and cheered with delight.
5. Talk more quietly!
6. Sergio and Felix waved to the crowd.
7. There go Lucy and Juan to the beach.
8. Was the dog or the cat scratching outside the door last night?
9. This small stream eventually flows into the St. Lawrence Seaway.
10. Swim fast and watch for sharks!

Check your answers on page 27 in the Answer Key for Book One. If you correctly identified the subjects and verbs in 8 of 10 sentences, go to Subskill 9B. If not, ask your instructor for help.

Subskill 9B: Identifying Subject + Action Verb + Direct Object Sentences

When you complete this subskill, you will be able to identify a subject + action verb + direct object sentence pattern. You will be able to identify when this kind of sentence is a complete sentence.

The meaning of some sentences isn't complete with only a subject and an action verb. Look at these examples:

S   V

Stan locked _____.

S   V

Patricia met _____.

You need to put some words in the blanks to make these complete sentences. You need to tell <u>what</u> Stan locked and <u>whom</u> Patricia met. Words that answer these questions are called direct objects. **A direct object is a noun or pronoun that tells who or what received the action in the sentence.** You can always tell if a word is a direct object by asking the questions "What?" or "Whom?" after the action verb. We'll fill in the blanks in the examples to show how this works.

S   V

Stan locked the door.

locked <u>what</u>?   the door

S   V

Patricia met the boss.

met <u>whom</u>?   the boss

The noun <u>door</u> is the direct object of the action verb <u>locked</u>. The noun <u>boss</u> is the direct object of the action verb <u>met</u>. We could have used pronouns as direct objects in these sentences.

S   V

Stan locked it.

locked <u>what</u>?   it

S   V

Patricia met him.

met <u>whom</u>?   him

The pronouns <u>it</u> and <u>him</u> are now the direct objects of the action verbs.

Compound Direct Objects

In Subskill 9A, you saw how we could add adjectives, adverbs, and prepositional phrases to the subject + action verb sentence pattern. You also saw how any part of the pattern could be a compound. You can add words to the subject + action verb + direct object pattern in the same ways. In these examples, we'll mark the direct objects <u>DO</u>.

	S S V DO
COMPOUND SUBJECT:	Fred and Mary brought wine.

                                    S   V   V   DO

COMPOUND VERB: He ironed and folded the shirts.

                                    S   V   DO

COMPOUND DIRECT OBJECT: Sara hated the movie and the

                                    DO

                                    dinner.

Now, let's add adjectives, adverbs, and a prepositional phrase to one of these sentences.

    S   S   Adv   V   Adv Adj DO
Fred and Mary thoughtfully brought a very good wine

Prep. Phrase

⌒

to the party.

As you can see in this sentence, a direct object does not always come right after the action verb. One or more adjectives can be added to describe the direct object. They will come between the action verb and the direct object. And the direct object is not always the last word in the sentence. One or more prepositional phrases can come after the direct object.

In sentences with a compound action verb, each verb can have its own separate direct object. Look at this example:

    S   S   V
Dr. Erskine and Dr. Reed examined the x–rays and

    V
diagnosed the illness.

Here, a compound subject is followed by the action verbs <u>examined</u> and <u>diagnosed</u>. To find the direct object of the first action verb, ask "examined what?" The direct object of <u>examined</u> is <u>x–rays</u>. Next, ask "diagnosed what?" to find the direct object of the second action verb. The noun <u>illness</u> is the direct object of the action verb <u>diagnosed</u>. You can see from this example that you can have a different direct object for each of the action verbs. So, you need to ask who or what received the action for every verb in the sentence.

Don't be confused when the subject and action verb are part of a question. Just remember to ask the questions "What?" and "Whom?" after all the words in the verb phrase to find the direct object.

.V S V DO
Are you watching television?

are watching <u>what</u>?   television

As you saw in Subskill 9A, not all action verbs have direct objects. But some action verb sentences would not be complete sentences without a direct object.

Try your skill at identifying the parts of complete sentences with the subject + action verb + direct object pattern in the following exercise. For each sentence, try asking yourself, "Would I understand the meaning of this sentence without the direct object?" The following exercise will also check your understanding of subject + action verb patterns. REMEMBER: a direct object answers "Whom?" or "What?" after an action verb. An adverb or a prepositional phrase that acts as an adverb answers "How?", "When?", or "Where?" after an action verb. Be careful not to confuse a direct object with another word that follows an action verb.

Exercise for Subskill 9B

Read sentences 1–10 on page 141 and do the following:

- Write all subjects in the column labeled <u>Subjects</u>. If the subject is understood, write <u>you</u> in parentheses in this column.

- Write all verbs in the column labeled <u>Verbs</u>.

- Write all direct objects in the column labeled <u>Direct Objects</u>.

- If any of the subjects, verbs, or direct objects are compound, include the conjunctions.

Review your work to be sure you have completed each step.

	Subjects	Verbs	Direct Objects
EXAMPLE:	someone	threw	snowball
1.			
2.			
3.			
4.			
5.			

	Subjects	Verbs	Direct Objects
6.			
7.			
8.			
9.			
10.			

EXAMPLE: Someone threw a snowball at me.

1. Francine wrote a letter to me.
2. Play some music for us.
3. The dog ran outside.
4. He and I robbed a bank and split the money.
5. The man in the long coat walked home.
6. Have you seen any stray animals recently?
7. Marge opened the door and greeted the doctor.
8. When did Bruce Jenner win his gold medals?
9. Don't lose that key!
10. Like Gandhi, Martin Luther King, Jr. preached and practiced nonviolence.

Check your answers on page 28 in the Answer Key for Book One. If you correctly identified the subjects, verbs, and direct objects in all 10 sentences, go to Subskill 9C. If not, do the Supplemental Exercise for Subskill 9B.

Supplemental Exercise for Subskill 9B

Some sentences have a pattern of subject + action verb + direct object (S + V + DO). The direct object is a noun or pronoun that tells who or what received the action in the sentence. You can identify direct objects in sentences by asking the questions "What?" and "Whom?" after the action verb. A word that answers one of these questions is a direct object. Look at this example:

Prep. Phrase

S   V   DO   ⌒

Denise kissed Manny on the cheek.

Here, the direct object answers the question "kissed whom?" A prepositional phrase comes after the direct object. The phrase does the job of an adverb by answering the question "Where?" about the verb <u>kissed</u>.

You can add adjectives, adverbs, and prepositional phrases to the basic sentence pattern. And any part of the pattern can be a compound. Be careful with sentences that have compound verbs. Each verb can have its own direct object.

<pre>
              S   V   DO   V   DO
</pre>
The thief mugged the man and stole his wallet.

This sentence has a compound verb: <u>mugged</u> and <u>stole</u>. To find the direct objects, ask:

mugged whom?   the <u>man</u>

stole what?   his <u>wallet</u>

Not all action verb sentences have to have direct objects to be complete. Some sentences have the pattern you studied in Subskill 9A: subject + action verb. Just remember to ask the questions "Whom?" and "What?" after an action verb. You will find the direct object if there is one.

Read sentences 1–10 on page 143 and do the following:

- Write all subjects in the column labeled <u>Subjects</u>. If the subject is understood, write <u>you</u> in parentheses in this column.

- Write all verbs in the column labeled <u>Verbs</u>.

- Write all direct objects in the column labeled <u>Direct</u> <u>Objects</u>.

- If any of the subjects, verbs, or direct objects are compound, include the conjunctions.

Review your work to be sure you have completed each step.

	Subjects	Verbs	Direct Objects
EXAMPLE:	mother	kissed and sent	son him
1.			
2.			
3.			
4.			
5.			
6.			
7.			

	Subjects	Verbs	Direct Objects
8.			
9.			
10.			

EXAMPLE: The mother kissed her son and sent him to school.

1. Howard selected a gift and wrapped it.
2. Please sign this agreement.
3. Heather painted the fence.
4. Did Anne or Ada cross the street alone?
5. Norma and Earl sold their car and bought a van.
6. The Canadian ambassador shook the Prime Minister's hand.
7. Will you give that book to me?
8. The front desk clerk tripped on the rug and fell.
9. Martha and Ray would never have found the cabin without a map.
10. Light the oven.

Check your answers on page 28 in the Answer Key for Book One. If you correctly identified the subjects, verbs, and direct objects in 8 of 10 sentences, go to Subskill 9C. If not, ask your instructor for help.

Subskill 9C: Identifying Subject + Action Verb + Indirect Object + Direct Object Sentences

When you complete this subskill, you will be able to identify a subject + action verb + indirect object + direct object sentence pattern. You will be able to identify when this kind of sentence is a complete sentence.

In the first two subskills, you learned to identify the parts of complete sentences. Some sentences need only a subject plus an action verb (or verb phrase) to be complete:

S   V

Bob is reading.

Sometimes you need to tell "whom" or "what" received the action in the sentence to be complete. That is, sometimes you need a direct object. Although the first sentence about Bob is complete without a direct object, you could add one:

        S   V   DO
    Bob is reading a book.

You can add words to describe any part of the basic sentence pattern. These words may be adjectives, adverbs, or prepositional phrases:

        S V Adv   V   Adv Adj DO
    Bob is carefully reading a very good book

        Prep. Phrase
    ⏝⏝⏝⏝⏝⏝
    about tropical fish.

But look at the following sentence. What kind of word is children?

        S   V   DO
    Bob is reading the children a book.

You know that the word children is a noun—not an adjective or an adverb. And it is not part of a prepositional phrase—there is no preposition in the sentence. But it can't be called a direct object either. A direct object answers the questions "Whom?" or "What?" after the verb. You can read a book, but you can't read children.

The word children is doing a different kind of job in the sentence. It answers the questions "To whom?" or "For whom?" about the action. Nouns or pronouns that answer these questions are called **indirect objects.** Let's look at some more examples of words that do the job of an indirect object. We'll mark the subjects S, the verbs V, the indirect objects IO, and the direct objects DO.

              S   V   IO   DO
           Mel gave Bert the money.

        S   V   IO   DO
     (You)   Please buy me a ticket.

           V   S   V   IO   DO
           Did you tell José everything?

In each of these sentences, the indirect object tells "to whom" or "for whom" the action is done. From these examples, you can see that commands and questions can have indirect objects. You can identify direct and indirect objects by asking the questions you have learned. It is usually best to find the direct object first. We'll use the questions with the examples you just read.

Mel gave Bert the money.

gave <u>what</u>?   the money   (direct object)

<u>to whom</u>?   Bert   (indirect object)

Please buy me a ticket.

buy <u>what</u>?   a ticket   (direct object)

<u>for whom</u>?   me   (indirect object)

Did you tell José everything?

did tell <u>what</u>?   everything   (direct object)

<u>to whom</u>?   José   (indirect object)

You know that direct objects can answer the question "Whom?" about the action. But what would happen if we used that question with the sentences you just read?

gave <u>whom</u>?   Bert?

buy <u>whom</u>?   me?

did tell <u>whom</u>?   José?

You need to think about the meanings of the action verbs. In the first sentence, Mel isn't giving Bert to anyone. In the second sentence, I'm not actually asking someone to buy me. I can't be bought. And what about the action verb <u>tell</u>? What you can tell—or speak with words— is a thing. You can't speak a person.

There are two clues you can use to check whether a noun or pronoun is an indirect object.

Clue 1:   If the word is an indirect object, you can add <u>to</u> or <u>for</u> to it and place the words at the end of the sentence. The new sentence will have the same meaning as the old one.

Mel gave the money <u>to</u> Bert.

Please buy a ticket <u>for</u> me.

Did you tell everything <u>to</u> José?

The sentence won't make sense if you add <u>to</u> or <u>for</u> in front of the direct object.

Mel gave Bert <u>to</u> the money.

Please buy me <u>for</u> a ticket.

Did you tell José <u>to</u> everything?

Clue 2: In a sentence with two objects that are not joined by a conjunction (<u>and</u>, <u>but</u>, <u>or</u>, <u>nor</u>), the first is the indirect object and the second is the direct object.

S   V IO   DO
He asked me the way.

S   V IO   DO
Brian paid her the money.

S   V IO   DO
She gave Harry a hint.

If the sentence contains only two objects and the objects are joined by a conjunction, the two objects are direct objects.

S   V   DO   DO
Lucy had some cold pizza and a beer for breakfast.

Although there are two objects in this sentence, the first one is not an indirect object. The conjunction <u>and</u> joins the two objects and makes them a compound direct object.

Compound Indirect Objects

You already know that sentences can have compound subjects, compound verbs, and compound direct objects. Sentences can also have compound indirect objects.

S   V   IO   IO   DO
Mr. Egan gave the secretary and me a raise.

gave <u>what</u>?   a raise (direct object)

<u>to whom</u>?   the secretary and me (indirect objects)

V IO   IO   DO
Please write him and me an excuse.

write <u>what</u>?   an excuse (direct object)

<u>for whom</u>?   him and me (indirect objects)

In this sentence, the subject <u>you</u> is understood. The sentence still has the S + V + IO + DO pattern.

Look at this pattern in questions:

Will you teach her and me Greek?

Turn the question around to see the pattern:

S   V   IO   IO DO
You will teach her and me Greek.

teach <u>what</u>?   Greek   (direct object)

<u>to whom</u>?   her and me   (indirect objects)

In sentences with a compound verb, each verb can have its own separate indirect and direct objects.

<pre>
      S   V   IO DO   V   IO   DO
</pre>
She bought me dinner but gave my friend her love.

You can also add adjectives, adverbs, and prepositional phrases to describe the indirect object.

<pre>
      S   V   IO DO
</pre>
She told the man a joke.

<pre>
      S   V   Adv   Adj   IO   Prep. Phrase
</pre>
She told the extremely handsome man in the corner

Prep. Phrase   DO

of the room a joke.

Now, try your skill at identifying the parts of complete sentences with the subject + action verb + indirect object + direct object pattern in the following exercise. This exercise will also check your understanding of S + V and S + V + DO sentence patterns.

Exercise for Subskill 9C

Read sentences 1–10 on page 148 and do the following:

- Write all subjects in the column labeled <u>Subjects</u>. If the subject is understood, write <u>you</u> in parentheses in this column.

- Write all verbs in the column labeled <u>Verbs</u>.

- Write all indirect objects in the column labeled <u>Indirect</u> <u>Objects</u>.

- Write all direct objects in the column labeled <u>Direct</u> <u>Objects</u>.

- If any of the subjects, verbs, indirect objects, or direct objects are compound, include the conjunctions.

Review your work to be sure you have completed each step.

	Subjects	Verbs	Indirect Objects	Direct Objects
EXAMPLE:	(you)	do give	it	thought
1.				

	Subjects	Verbs	Indirect Objects	Direct Objects
2.				
3.				
4.				
5.				
6.				
7.				
8.				
9.				
10.				

EXAMPLE: Don't give it a second thought!

1. My sister and brother taught me the alphabet and numbers.
2. My husband and I promised my sister and her husband an anniversary party.
3. Will you buy me some aspirin for my cold?
4. Give us our tickets.
5. Throw the ball.
6. Did Carol pay you the money?
7. Her son brought flowers for Mother's Day.
8. Speak slowly and distinctly.
9. Ruth gave Bob ten dollars and me five dollars.
10. Are you listening to me?

Check your answers on page 29 in the Answer Key for Book One. If you correctly identified the subjects, verbs, indirect objects, and direct objects in all 10 sentences, go to Subskill 9D. If not, do the Supplemental Exercise for Subskill 9C.

Supplemental Exercise for Subskill 9C

You have now studied the three patterns used to make complete sentences with action verbs.

S + V: Rick writes.

S + V + DO: Rick writes letters.

S + V + IO + DO: Rick writes Kathy letters.

You can find the direct object by asking "Whom?" or "What?" after the verb. The noun <u>letters</u> is a direct object in the second and third sentences about Rick.

You can find the indirect object by asking the questions "To whom?" or "For whom?" The noun <u>Kathy</u> is an indirect object in the last sentence about Rick.

You can check to see whether a word is an indirect object. All you have to do is put the words <u>to</u> or <u>for</u> in front of the noun or pronoun and move the words to the end of the sentence. If the sentence makes sense, the noun or pronoun is an indirect object.

Rick writes letters <u>to</u> Kathy.

You also can add adjectives, adverbs, and prepositional phrases to any sentence. And you can make any sentence part a compound.

S   Adv   V   Adj   IO   Adj
Rick always writes his dear Kathy long

        Prep. Phrase   Prep. Phrase
DO
letters from his new home in Vermont but

Adv   V   IO   Adj   DO
only sends me short postcards.

In this example, there is a compound verb: <u>writes</u> and <u>sends</u>. And each verb has its own indirect and direct objects.

If the pattern is used to make a command or a request, the subject is not usually written. The subject is understood to be <u>you</u>. The command or request is still complete without writing the subject <u>you</u>.

     S   V   IO   DO
(You)   Tell me the truth.

In questions, part of the verb phrase comes in front of the subject.

V   S   V   IO   DO
Are you telling me the truth?

Read sentences 1–10 on page 151 and do the following:

- Write all subjects in the column labeled <u>Subjects</u>. If the subject is understood, write <u>you</u> in parentheses in this column.

- Write all verbs in the column labeled <u>Verbs</u>.

- Write all indirect objects in the column labeled <u>Indirect</u> <u>Objects</u>.

- Write all direct objects in the column labeled <u>Direct</u> <u>Objects</u>.

- If any of the subjects, verbs, indirect objects, or direct objects are compound, include the conjunctions.

Review your work to be sure you have completed each step.

	Subjects	Verbs	Indirect Objects	Direct Objects
EXAMPLE:	neighbor	had told	him and me	story
1.				
2.				
3.				
4.				
5.				
6.				
7.				
8.				
9.				
10.				

EXAMPLE: A neighbor had told him and me the whole story.

1. Give your cat food and water in the morning.
2. The doctor gave me a prescription.
3. The pitcher quickly threw the ball.
4. Will you help Jack with his homework?
5. Where are you going?
6. Did you loan him some money?
7. Mr. Jones asked me a question but didn't hear my answer.
8. Follow that cab!
9. Elena will fly to New York for Christmas.
10. Speak softly and carry a big stick.

Check your answers on pages 29 and 30 in the Answer Key for Book One. If you correctly identified the subjects, verbs, indirect objects, and direct objects in 8 of 10 sentences, go to Subskill 9D. If not, ask your instructor for help.

Subskill 9D: Identifying Subject + Linking Verb + Subject Complement Sentences

When you complete this subskill, you will be able to identify a subject + linking verb + subject complement sentence pattern. You will be able to identify when this kind of sentence is complete.

In the first three subskills in this skill unit, you learned to identify the patterns of sentences that contain action verbs. But action verbs are only one of the kinds of verbs we use in English. In Skill Unit 5, you learned to identify another kind of verb—the linking verb. As a review, here is a list of the most common linking verbs:

Common Linking Verbs

am	were	appear	feel
is	will be	become	look
are	has/have been	grow	smell
was	had been	remain	sound
		seem	taste

Linking verbs can be used to link the subject to a noun or pronoun that renames the subject. Or they can link the subject to an adjective that describes the subject.

<pre>
                                         V
       LINK TO NOUN: Tania is a salesperson.
                                                   V
       LINK TO PRONOUN: The best salesperson will be she.
                                     V
       LINK TO ADJECTIVE: She seemed happy.
</pre>

In the first sentence, the verb <u>is</u> links the subject <u>Tania</u> to the noun <u>salesperson</u>. The noun <u>salesperson</u> renames the subject. In the second sentence, the verb <u>will be</u> links the pronoun <u>she</u> to the subject <u>salesperson</u>. The pronoun <u>she</u> renames the subject. In the last sentence, the verb <u>seemed</u> links the adjective <u>happy</u> to the subject <u>she</u>. The adjective <u>happy</u> describes the subject.

Nouns, pronouns, and adjectives that come after linking verbs are called <u>subject complements</u>. They complement the subject by renaming or describing the subject.

You can do all the things to linking verb sentences that you have been doing to action verb sentences. You can add adjectives, adverbs, and prepositional phrases. And you can make any part of the pattern a compound. In the examples, we'll mark the subjects <u>S</u>, the linking verbs <u>LV</u>, and the subject complements <u>SC</u>.

<pre>
            S   LV   SC
      The man was a teacher.

                       Prep. Phrase
       Adj S   ⌒‿‿‿‿‿⌒   LV   Adv
      The old man across the street was a particularly

                      Prep. Phrase
       Adj   SC   ⌒‿‿‿‿‿⌒
      good teacher in my school.
</pre>

In the second sentence, we added an adjective and a prepositional phrase to describe the subject <u>man</u>. The noun <u>teacher</u> is the subject complement. Since the subject complement is a noun, we can describe the noun with an adjective—<u>good</u>. To describe the adjective <u>good</u>, we must use an adverb. In this sentence, we used the adverb <u>particularly</u> to describe <u>good</u>. And finally, we added a prepositional phrase to tell "Which one?" about the subject complement <u>teacher</u>.

When the subject complement is an adjective, be careful in choosing words to describe the adjective. Remember, you must use an adverb to describe an adjective. And remember that a subject complement that describes the subject must always be an adjective.

<pre>
            S   V   SC
      The dinner smells good.

            S   V   Adv   SC
      The dinner smells awfully good.
</pre>

Questions can also have the S + LV + SC pattern. Look at these examples:

<pre>
       LV   S   LV   SC
      Will Orville be the chairperson?
</pre>

Now add a prepositional phrase:

<pre>
                                    Prep. Phrase
       LV   S   LV   SC   ‿‿‿‿‿‿‿‿‿‿‿‿‿
      Will Orville be the chairperson of our committee?
</pre>

To find the subject and verb, rewrite the question as a statement:

<pre>
                                    Prep. Phrase
       S   LV   SC   ‿‿‿‿‿‿‿‿‿‿‿‿‿
      Orville will be the chairperson of our committee.
</pre>

Compound Subject Complements

You can have compound subjects, verbs, and subject complements:

<pre>
        S   S   LV SC
      Tori and Heather Lee are happy.
</pre>

<pre>
        S   LV   LV SC
      The vegetables smell and taste good.
</pre>

<pre>
        S   LV   SC   LV SC
      Kitty Steele feels feverish and looks ill.
</pre>

<pre>
        S   LV SC   SC
      Paulette Reed is tall and thin.
</pre>

Note that in the sentence with compound linking verbs, each verb has its own separate subject complement.

Remember: some verbs can be used either as action verbs or as linking verbs.

    (1) She <u>felt</u> her ankle.

    (2) She <u>felt</u> sick.

In sentence 1, the word <u>felt</u> is an action verb. It tells what she did. <u>Ankle</u> is a direct object that tells "what" she felt.

In sentence 2, <u>felt</u> is a linking verb. It links the subject <u>she</u> to the adjective <u>sick</u>, which describes <u>she</u>.

If you are not sure whether a word is an action verb or a linking verb, try to replace it with a form of the verb <u>be</u> or <u>seem</u>. If the sentence still makes sense, the word is a linking verb. If not, the word is an action verb.

(1) a. She <u>felt</u> her ankle.

b. She <u>was</u> her ankle.

Sentence 1b doesn't make sense. Therefore, <u>felt</u> is an action verb in this sentence.

(2) a. She <u>felt</u> sick.

b. She <u>was</u> sick.

Sentence 2b makes sense. Therefore, <u>felt</u> is a linking verb in this sentence.

Now try your skill at identifying the parts of complete sentences with the subject + linking verb + subject complement pattern. The following exercise will also check your understanding of action verb sentence patterns.

Exercise for Subskill 9D

Read sentences 1–10 on page 155 and do the following:

- Write all subjects in the column labeled <u>Subjects</u>. If the subject is understood, write <u>you</u> in parentheses in this column.

- Write all verbs in the column labeled <u>Verbs</u>.

- Write all indirect objects in the column labeled <u>Indirect Objects</u>.

- Write all direct objects in the column labeled <u>Direct Objects</u>.

- Write all subject complements in the column labeled <u>Subject Complements</u>.

- If any of the subjects, verbs, indirect objects, direct objects, or subject complements are compound, include the conjunctions.

Review your work to be sure you have completed each step.

	Subjects	Verbs	Indirect Objects	Direct Objects	Subject Complements
EXAMPLES:	Debbie	bought	me	shirt	
	Debbie and Pat	are			friends
1.					

	Subjects	Verbs	Indirect Objects	Direct Objects	Subject Complements
2.					
3.					
4.					
5.					
6.					
7.					
8.					
9.					
10.					

EXAMPLES: Debbie bought me a new shirt.

Debbie and Pat are my friends.

1. Were their plans firm?
2. In autumn, the leaves turn gold and red.
3. Save me a piece of cake.
4. Amy and Alice looked well and seemed relaxed after their vacation.
5. She will become a doctor after graduation.
6. This past week, I have been very happy.
7. I have been visiting a friend today.
8. The garden smelled fragrant.
9. Sol looked angry and tense.
10. Simon looked quickly behind him.

Check your answers on page 30 in the Answer Key for Book One. If you correctly identified the subjects, verbs, indirect objects, direct objects, and subject complements in all 10 sentences, go to the Self–Check. If not, do the Supplemental Exercise for Subskill 9D.

Supplemental Exercise for Subskill 9D

All sentences with linking verbs follow the pattern subject + linking verb + subject complement. The subject complement can be a noun or pronoun that renames the subject. Or it can be an adjective that describes the subject. Look at these examples.

                         S LV   SC

LINK TO NOUN: She is a teacher.

                        S LV SC

LINK TO PRONOUN: I am she.

                        S LV SC

LINK TO ADJECTIVE: She is pretty.

You can add adjectives, adverbs, and prepositional phrases to this pattern. Just make sure you describe adjectives used as subject complements with adverbs.

      S LV   Adv   SC
She is extremely pretty.

                                  Prep. Phrase
      S LV   Adj   SC
She is an excellent teacher in our school.

You can invert the sentence pattern in questions.

        LV S SC
        Are you she?

And any part of the pattern can be a compound.

      S   S LV   SC
You and she are my friends.

      S LV   SC   SC
She is my friend and companion.

      S LV SC   LV SC
He felt better and looked rested.

Read sentences 1–10 on pages 157 and 158 and do the following:

- Write all subjects in the column labeled Subjects. If the subject is understood, write you in parentheses in this column.

- Write all verbs in the column labeled Verbs.

- Write all indirect objects in the column labeled Indirect Objects.

- Write all direct objects in the column labeled Direct Objects.

- Write all subject complements in the column labeled Subject Complements.

- If any of the subjects, verbs, indirect objects, direct objects, or subject complements are compound, include the conjunctions.

Review your work to be sure you have completed each step.

	Subjects	Verbs	Indirect Objects	Direct Objects	Subject Complements
EXAMPLES:	air	smelled and tasted			fishy salty
	(you)	do follow		me	
1.					
2.					
3.					
4.					
5.					
6.					
7.					
8.					
9.					
10.					

EXAMPLES: The sea air smelled fishy and tasted salty.
Don't follow me!

1. Is she that happy?
2. The bride threw me the bouquet of flowers.
3. Mary is a reliable worker and a good organizer.
4. This winter should be mild.
5. The parrot flew off his perch and out of his cage.
6. I tasted the meat but didn't like it.
7. It tasted very bland to me.
8. I hate English but like math.

9. The tall man by the door is my math instructor.
10. The side of that mountain is very steep and smooth.

Check your answers on pages 30 and 31 in the Answer Key for Book One. If you correctly identified the subjects, verbs, indirect objects, direct objects, and subject complements in 8 of 10 sentences, go to the Self–Check. If not, ask your instructor for help.

SELF-CHECK: SKILL UNIT 9

Read sentences 1–15 on page 159 and do the following:

- Write all subjects in the column labeled Subjects. If the subject is understood, write you in parentheses in this column.
- Write all verbs in the column labeled Verbs.
- Write all indirect objects in the column labeled Indirect Objects.
- Write all direct objects in the column labeled Direct Objects.
- Write all subject complements in the column labeled Subject Complements.
- If any of the subjects, verbs, indirect objects, direct objects, or subject complements are compound, include the conjunctions.

Review your work to be sure you have completed each step.

	Subjects	Verbs	Indirect Objects	Direct Objects	Subject Complements
EXAMPLES:	popcorn	tastes			salty
	bird	flew			
1.					
2.					
3.					
4.					
5.					
6.					

	Subjects	Verbs	Indirect Objects	Direct Objects	Subject Complements
7.					
8.					
9.					
10.					
11.					
12.					
13.					
14.					
15.					

EXAMPLES: This popcorn tastes too salty.

A bird flew into the apartment.

1. I wrote her a long letter.
2. Doesn't her hair look great?
3. The ashtray fell and broke.
4. Don't forget Rosanna's birthday!
5. We have promised our daughter a new bike.
6. There goes the winner of the race.
7. Dan and Sheri are playing baseball at the park.
8. Mark fell and broke his leg.
9. Is that woman your sister?
10. Did you buy Henry or Tim a present?
11. I feel uncomfortable in these shoes.
12. Feel my forehead.
13. Bob and Sharon told me the whole story.
14. The only suspect in the room without an alibi was she.
15. I can promise them nothing.

Check your answers on pages 31 and 32 in the Answer Key for Book One. If you correctly answered 12 of 15 items, you have shown that you have mastered these skills. If not, ask your instructor for help.

Posttest
GRAMMAR FUNDAMENTALS

The following test will help you find out how much you have learned about grammar fundamentals. The test will also help you to see which English skills you need to review.

The test is divided into nine parts, one part for each unit in the book. You may want to take the test all at once or one unit at a time, depending on what you and your instructor decide. When you complete the test, check your answers in the Answer Key for Book One. Then turn to the Skills Correlation Chart on pages 174 and 175 and circle the number of any questions you missed. The chart will show you which parts of this book covered the English skills that gave you the most trouble. You should review the parts that match the questions that you missed.

Skill Unit 1: Identifying Nouns

Part A. Underline all the nouns, or naming words, you find in the following sentences.

EXAMPLE: <u>Donna</u> flew to <u>Hawaii</u> for her <u>vacation</u>.

1. Honesty is the best policy in this case.

2. After the fire, our family moved into an apartment on the same street.

3. Does your cousin need a ride to work tomorrow?

4. Matt dropped his glasses behind the couch.

Part B. In sentences 5–8 on pages 161 and 162, underline all the common nouns and capitalize all the proper nouns.

<pre>
                 S   R   S
</pre>
EXAMPLE: Will $am visit řebecca and her <u>brother</u> in $eptember?

5. Did ramona visit the golden gate bridge in san francisco?

6. My sister michele said that the clover leaf diner needs a waitress.

7. After dinner, joe studied english for two hours.

8. Does mr. perez still live on encino boulevard?

Part C. Some words serve as noun markers because they often come before common nouns. In the following sentences, circle the noun markers and underline the nouns.

EXAMPLE: Walt found a dollar under a seat on the bus.

9. Can the couple afford a new car as well as an armchair for the living room?

10. The movie was an adventure film about a soldier in the South American jungles.

11. The postman said the letter needed a stamp.

12. A bird flew into the bedroom this morning.

Answers appear on page 33 in the Answer Key for Book One.

Skill Unit 2:   Identifying Pronouns

Part A. Underline all the personal pronouns you find in the following sentences.

EXAMPLE: Gerry found the kitten, but she gave it to us.

1. Did you hear that they left without paying last month's bill?

2. We never told her that you needed help.

3. She was probably the only other person I told.

4. Did you ask him if he could watch the children tonight?

5. They asked me to put them to bed at 8:30.

Part B. Underline all the possessive pronouns you find in the following sentences.

EXAMPLE: We lost all our money at the casino.

6. My only son was killed in the war.

7. This shirt is mine. Yours is over there.

8. Can we borrow your flashlight? We forgot to bring ours.

9. His hair is much darker than hers.

10. There's more to this than their parents are willing to tell.

Part C.   In each of the following sentences, underline all the interrogative, demonstrative, and indefinite pronouns you find. Then, rewrite them on the lines below each sentence and write <u>interrogative</u>, <u>demonstrative</u>, or <u>indefinite</u> after each pronoun to identify what type it is.

EXAMPLE: <u>What</u> didn't you like about the movie?

_____What—interrogative_____

11. No one has claimed any of the money yet.

_____

_____

12. Which of these belongs to you?

_____

_____

13. Who is at the door?

_____

_____

14. I have just about everything I need to do the job.

_____

_____

15. That should be returned to somebody in the manufacturing division.

_____

_____

Answers appear on pages 33 and 34 in the Answer Key for Book One.

Skill Unit 3:   Identifying Action Verbs

Part A.   Underline all the action verbs you find in the following sentences.

EXAMPLE: <u>Put</u> Thelma's coat in the closet.

1.   I believe your version of the story.

2.   Please forget about it.

3.   I ran in the ten kilometer run on Saturday.

4.   This soup needs more salt.

Part B.   Underline the main verb and circle any helping verbs you find in the following sentences.

EXAMPLE: She (has) (been) <u>asking</u> about you all night.

5.   We were driving home late last night.

6.   We should have started earlier.

7.   Mrs. Thomas has watered our plants for us on several occasions.

8.   Chris had wanted a new car for a long time.

Part C.   A sentence can have more than one verb. Underline all the verbs or verb phrases in the following sentences.

EXAMPLE: Juan <u>weeded</u> the lawn and <u>planted</u> some vegetables.

9.   I can read the lesson and answer all the questions in about an hour.

10.   Allen cleaned his room and folded his clothes.

11.   Adrian and Lisa drove to the school and picked up the children.

12.   Peter set the table and then cooked the chicken.

Part D.   Verb phrases can be divided by other words in the sentence. Underline all the verbs and verb phrases in the following sentences. Do not underline words which are not part of the verb phrase.

EXAMPLE: We <u>have</u> never <u>watched</u> that program.

13.   Have you seen them today?

14.   Did we win the lottery?

15.   Does this tool make your work easier?

16. I do not want any dessert tonight.

Answers appear on page 34 in the Answer Key for Book One.

Skill Unit 4:   Identifying Subject–Verb Combinations

Part A.   Underline the subject of each sentence once and the verb twice.

EXAMPLE: <u>Tom</u> <u><u>has driven</u></u> across the country before.

1. We should have bought more paint.
2. The radio played loudly in the next room.
3. He called your office twice today.
4. The doctor will see you now.

Part B.   A sentence may have more than one subject or verb. In each of the following sentences, underline the subjects once and the verbs twice. Then, circle the words that connect the compound subject and compound verbs.

EXAMPLE: The <u>dog</u>(and)<u>cat</u> <u><u>growled</u></u>(and)<u><u>hissed</u></u> at each other.

5. The man and woman argued but then apologized.
6. The plumbing and the wiring will need repair work.
7. The sofa, chair, and table go over there.
8. Your aunt and uncle like the country but hate the city.

Part C.   In each of the following sentences, underline the subject once and the verb or verb phrase twice. If the subject is understood, write <u>you</u> in parentheses in the space after each sentence.

EXAMPLE: <u><u>Wait</u></u> for me at the theater.   ___(you)___

9. Go down two blocks and turn right.   _____
10. Turn on the television.   _____
11. We need bread and milk.   _____
12. Pick up some fresh fruit, too.   _____

Part D.   Each of the following sentences has a subject-verb combination in inverted order. Underline the subject once and the verb or verb phrase twice.

EXAMPLE: <u>Do</u> <u>you</u> <u>love</u> him?

13.   Here is the money for the tickets.

14.   In front of the house sat the most beautiful red car.

15.   There are several solutions to this problem.

16.   Do you need the car tonight?

Part E.   More complicated sentences may have more than one subject-verb combination. Find all the subject-verb combinations in the following sentences. Underline the subjects once and the verbs twice.

EXAMPLE: <u>You</u> <u>should give</u> me the money before <u>I</u> <u>leave</u>.

17.   Because we forgot our key, we waited for the building superintendent.

18.   I like fried chicken, but my friend likes roasted chicken.

19.   If you can wait a minute, I will go with you.

20.   I made the salad, and Michael set the table.

Part F.   Sometimes, words come between the subject and the verb in a sentence. See if you can find the subject-verb combinations in these sentences. Underline the subjects once and the verbs twice.

EXAMPLE: The <u>man</u> standing on the roof <u>keeps</u> pigeons.

21.   The house with the brown roof sold for $45,000.

22.   The mechanic looking under the hood of my car shook his head and whistled softly.

23.   The money for my vacation is going for car repairs this year.

24.   The house with the big front yard and beautiful flowers belongs to my grandfather.

Answers appear on pages 34 and 35 in the Answer Key for Book One.

Skill Unit 5:   Identifying Linking Verbs

Part A.   In the following sentences, the forms of the verb <u>be</u> are underlined. If the form of <u>be</u> is used as a linking verb, write <u>LV</u> in the blank and circle the word which renames the subject. If it is part of an action verb phrase, write <u>AV</u> in the blank.

EXAMPLE: Our car <u>is</u> the only (vehicle) on the road.   <u>LV</u>

1. It <u>will be</u> a four-hour drive by the time we get to
    St. Louis.   _____

2. She <u>was</u> not a very good student.   _____

3. The waiter <u>was</u> clearing the tables when we arrived.   _____

4. Eisenhower <u>was</u> President for eight years.   _____

5. They never had <u>been</u> seen here before.   _____

Part B.   In the following sentences, the forms of the verb <u>be</u> are under-lined. If the form of <u>be</u> is used as a linking verb, write <u>LV</u> in the blank and circle the word or words which describe the subject. If the form of <u>be</u> is part of an action verb phrase, write <u>AV</u> in the blank.

EXAMPLE: They <u>will be</u> (tired) after driving all night.   <u>LV</u>

6. <u>Will</u> you <u>be</u> coming over tonight?   _____

7. They <u>were</u> always suspicious of him.   _____

8. She <u>will be</u> driving our bus from now on.   _____

9. The day <u>was</u> dark and cold.   _____

10. Our phone bill <u>is</u> very high this month.   _____

Part C.   The verbs in the following sentences have been underlined. Read each sentence carefully. If the verb is used as a linking verb, write <u>LV</u> in the blank and circle the word or words which describe the subject of the sentence. If the verb is used as an action verb, write <u>AV</u> in the blank.

EXAMPLE: The doctor <u>felt</u> my pulse.   <u>AV</u>

11. This radio <u>sounds</u> terrible.   _____

12. He <u>tasted</u> the soup carefully.   _____

13. It <u>tasted</u> very good.   _____

14. The guard <u>sounded</u> the alarm at the gate.   _____

15. <u>Will</u> you <u>feel</u> different about it in the morning? _____

Answers appear on pages 35 and 36 in the Answer Key for Book One.

Skill Unit 6:   Identifying Adjectives

Part A.   In a sentence, an adjective can answer the questions "What kind?", "How much?", "How many?", or "Which one?" about a noun or a pronoun. Find all the adjectives in each of the following sentences.

Then, in the blank after each sentence, write the adjectives and the question each answers.

EXAMPLE: This movie has been seen by many people.

_____this—Which one?_____many—How many?_____

1.   This is my favorite chair.

_____

2.   Fourteen men returned from the long, hazardous expedition.

_____

3.   There is only a little water in this well.

_____

4.   I couldn't wait to see that exciting movie.

_____

5.   The shiny, new penny fascinated the two children.

_____

Part B.   Find all the adjectives in the following sentences. Underline them and draw an arrow to the word they describe.

EXAMPLE: Are you tired of this conversation?

6.   The fresh vegetables look crisp and delicious today.

7.   The airport, crowded and noisy, gave me a headache.

8.   The small, quiet girl waited beside the back door.

9.   Your large, ferocious dog is frightening those children.

10.   Please don't return damaged or soiled merchandise.

Answers appear on page 36 in the Answer Key for Book One.

Skill Unit 7:   Identifying Adverbs

Part A.   In a sentence, an adverb can answer the question "How?", "Where?", or "When?" about an action verb. Underline the adverbs in the following sentences. After each sentence, write the question that has been answered by the adverb.

EXAMPLE: We looked for you <u>everywhere</u>. <u>Where?</u>

1. We usually eat dinner at six. _____
2. Stop that immediately! _____
3. Are you staying here? _____
4. The child smiled sweetly. _____

Part B. Write the adverbs that are formed from the following adjectives.

	Adjective	Adverb
EXAMPLE:	total	_____totally_____
5.	careful	_____
6.	crazy	_____
7.	agreeable	_____
8.	honest	_____

Part C. In each of the following pairs of sentences, a word is shown in two different positions. Put an <u>X</u> in the blank after each sentence in which the word acts as an adverb modifying a form of the verb <u>lose</u>. Be sure that the word can modify only the verb <u>lose</u> and no other verb. Sometimes, you will need to put an <u>X</u> in both blanks.

EXAMPLE: Tom <u>just</u> lost his keys five minutes ago. <u>X</u>

Tom lost <u>just</u> his keys and nothing else. <u>X</u>

9. We <u>soon</u> lost sight of the boys. ____

We lost sight of the boys <u>soon</u>. ____

10. The poker player lost his money <u>steadily</u>. ____

The poker player <u>steadily</u> lost his money. ____

11. I <u>almost</u> lost a dollar, but I found it again. ____

I lost <u>almost</u> a dollar in change. ____

12. I will <u>usually</u> lose a bet with Laurie. ____

<u>Usually</u>, I will lose a bet with Laurie. ____

Part D.   Find all the adverbs in the following sentences. On the line that follows each sentence, write the adverbs and the word each modifies.

EXAMPLE: Morris stays at home too much.

_____ much—stays   too—much _____

13.   We must leave very soon.

_____

14.   Margaret left for work fairly early.

_____

15.   I could not see very well.

_____

16.   Toni has a rather loud voice.

_____

Answers appear on pages 36 and 37 in the Answer Key for Book One.

Skill Unit 8:   Identifying Prepositions and Conjunctions

Part A.   Find all the prepositional phrases in each of the following sentences and circle them. Then, underline the preposition once and the object of the preposition twice.

EXAMPLE: They drove slowly (past the school.)

1.   Despite the recent rains, the lake was still below normal level.

2.   He stood beneath her window and called to her.

3.   You can't open the door without a key.

4.   You are acting like a child.

5.   Before the program, he announced he would be leaving in a month.

6.   Since June he has not been at work.

7.   The book is in the kitchen on the table or above the refrigerator.

8. We often get orders for that item.

Part B. Underline the conjunctions in each of the following sentences. Then, in the space following each sentence, tell whether the conjunction connects word to word, phrase to phrase, or statement to statement.

EXAMPLE: Buying a car can be expensive, <u>so</u> you need to shop carefully.

_____statement to statement_____

9. You may need a car, but only have a certain amount you can spend for it.

_____

10. Don't let a pushy or manipulating salesman convince you to spend more than you planned.

_____

11. Visit several dealers and take notes on the various cars.

_____

12. Some cars look acceptable, yet they have hidden defects.

_____

13. Take a car for a road test and try it under different driving conditions.

_____

14. How does it handle in city traffic and on highways?

_____

15. Is the steering aligned, or does the car stray to one side of the road?

_____

16. Check all the features of the car thoroughly, so you can be sure you are getting the best product for your money.

_____

Answers appear on pages 37 and 38 in the Answer Key for Book One.

Skill Unit 9:   Identifying Simple Sentences

Part A. In each of the following sentences, write S over each subject and V over each verb. If the subject is understood, write you in parentheses in the blank after the sentence.

              V
EXAMPLE: Dance with me.   (you)

1. The bank is across the street from City Hall. _____

2. The plane will land in twenty minutes. _____

3. Wait for me! _____

4. Suddenly, she slipped and fell into the mud puddle. _____

5. Are you staying at home this weekend? _____

Part B. In each of the following sentences, write S over each subject, V over each verb, and DO over each direct object. If the subject is understood, write you in parentheses in the blank after the sentence.

           S   V DO
EXAMPLE: I often see her in the supermarket. _____

6. We took flowers to our friend in the hospital. _____

7. Fold your clothes and put them away. _____

8. Did you leave a note on the door for him? _____

9. The door at the back of the room was locked from the outside.

_____

10. We stripped the old finish and repainted the table. _____

Part C. In each of the following sentences, write S over each subject, V over each verb, DO over each direct object, and IO over each indirect object. If the subject is understood, write you in parentheses in the blank after the sentence.

           V S V IO   DO
EXAMPLE: Could you tell us the name of your doctor? _____

11. They bought a housewarming gift for their best friends.

_____

12. The post office would not give him the new address. _____

13. Will you forward me my mail? _____

14. The lost children sat and cried softly. _____

15. Send them any damaged merchandise from past shipments.

_____

Part D.   In each of the following sentences, write S̲ over each subject, V̲ over each verb, D̲O̲ over each direct object, I̲O̲ over each indirect object, and S̲C̲ over each subject complement. If the subject is understood, write y̲o̲u̲ in parentheses in the blank after the sentence.

                    S   V   SC   SC
EXAMPLE: The water was clear and cold. _____

16. She seemed depressed after the accident. _____

17. My father was a tall and handsome man. _____

18. This coat is too small for you. _____

19. I felt my bruised leg gently. _____

20. He felt much better after a good night's sleep. _____

Answers appear on page 38 in the Answer Key for Book One.

Skills Correlation Chart for Posttest

After you check your answers, look at the following chart. Circle the numbers of any questions you missed. Then review the subskill in which the skills for the questions you missed are explained.

		QUESTION NUMBERS	SUBSKILL NUMBERS	SUBSKILL NAME	PAGE NUMBERS
Skill Unit One	IDENTIFYING NOUNS	1 2 3 4 5 6 7 8 9 10 11 12	1A 1B 1C	Identifying Words That Name Identifying Common and Proper Nouns Identifying Common Nouns Using Noun Markers	pages 17–21 pages 21–23 pages 23–26
		If you correctly answered 8 or fewer questions, you should review the subskills in Unit One for the questions you missed. If you correctly answered 9 or more of the questions in Unit One, go to Skill Unit Two.			
Skill Unit Two	IDENTIFYING PRONOUNS	1 2 3 4 5 6 7 8 9 10 11 12 13 14 15	2A 2B 2C	Identifying Personal Pronouns Identifying Possessive Pronouns Identifying Interrogative, Demonstrative, and Indefinite Pronouns	pages 29–34 pages 34–38 pages 39–42
		If you correctly answered 11 or fewer questions, you should review the subskills in Unit Two for the questions you missed. If you correctly answered 12 or more of the questions in Unit Two, go to Skill Unit Three			
Skill Unit Three	IDENTIFYING ACTION VERBS	1 2 3 4 5 6 7 8 9 10 11 12 13 14 15 16	3A 3B 3C 3D	Identifying Action Verbs in Sentences Identifying Verb Phrases, Main Verbs, and Helping Verbs Identifying Compound Verbs Identifying the Verbs in a Divided Verb Phrase	pages 45–49 pages 50–52 pages 52–54 pages 54–55
		If you correctly answered 11 or fewer questions, you should review the subskills in Unit Three for the questions you missed. If you correctly answered 12 or more of the questions in Unit Three, go to Skill Unit Four.			
Skill Unit Four	IDENTIFYING SUBJECT-VERB COMBINATIONS	1 2 3 4 5 6 7 8 9 10 11 12 13 14 15 16 17 18 19 20 21 22 23 24	4A 4B 4C 4D 4E 4F	Locating Subjects and Verbs in Sentences Identifying Compound Subjects and Compound Verbs Identifying Understood Subjects Identifying Subject-Verb Combinations in Inverted Sentences Identifying Sentences That Contain More Than One Subject-Verb Combination Identifying Subject-Verb Combinations When Words Come Between the Subject and the Verb	pages 58–62 pages 62–65 pages 66–68 pages 68–71 pages 71–75 pages 75–78
		If you correctly answered 18 or fewer questions, you should review the subskills in Unit Four for the questions you missed. If you correctly answered 19 or more of the questions in Unit Four, go to Skill Unit Five.			
Skill Unit Five	IDENTIFYING LINKING VERBS	1 2 3 4 5 6 7 8 9 10 11 12 13 14 15	5A 5B 5C	Recognizing That a Linking Verb Can Link the Subject to a Word That Renames the Subject Recognizing That a Linking Verb Can Link the Subject to a Describing Word Identifying Linking Verbs Other Than Be	pages 80–83 pages 83–85 pages 85–88
		If you correctly answered 11 or fewer questions, you should review the subskills in Unit Five for the questions you missed. If you correctly answered 12 or more of the questions in Unit Five, go to Skill Unit Six.			

		QUESTION NUMBERS	SUBSKILL NUMBER	SUBSKILL NAME	PAGE NUMBERS
Skill Unit Six	IDENTIFYING ADJECTIVES	1 2 3 4 5 6 7 8 9 10	6A 6B	Identifying the Use of Adjectives Identifying the Placement of Adjectives	pages 90–95 pages 95–98
		If you correctly answered 7 or fewer questions, you should review the subskills in Unit Six for the questions you missed. If you correctly answered 8 or more of the questions in Unit Six, go to Skill Unit Seven.			
Skill Unit Seven	IDENTIFYING ADVERBS	1 2 3 4 5 6 7 8 9 10 11 12 13 14 15 16	7A 7B 7C 7D	Identifying the Use of Adverbs to Describe Action Verbs Spelling Adverbs Correctly Identifying the Placement of Adverbs Identifying the Use of Adverbs to Describe Adjectives and Adverbs	pages 101–104 pages 104–108 pages 108–110 pages 110–115
		If you correctly answered 11 or fewer questions, you should review the subskills in Unit Seven for the questions you missed If you correctly answered 12 or more of the questions in Unit Seven, go to Skill Unit Eight.			
Skill Unit Eight	IDENTIFYING PREPOSITIONS AND CONJUNCTIONS	1 2 3 4 5 6 7 8 9 10 11 12 13 14 15 16	8A 8B	Identifying the Use of Prepositions Identifying the Use of Conjunctions	pages 119–123 pages 123–127
		If you correctly answered 11 or fewer questions, you should review the subskills in Unit Eight for the questions you missed. If you correctly answered 12 or more of the questions in Unit Eight, go to Skill Unit Nine.			
Skill Unit Nine	IDENTIFYING SIMPLE SENTENCES	1 2 3 4 5 6 7 8 9 10 11 12 13 14 15 16 17 18 19 20	9A 9B 9C 9D	Identifying Subject + Action Verb Sentences Identifying Subject + Action Verb + Direct Object Sentences Identifying Subject + Action Verb + Indirect Object + Direct Object Sentences Identifying Subject + Linking Verb + Subject Complement Sentences	pages 131–137 pages 138–143 pages 143–151 pages 151–158
		If you correctly answered 15 or fewer questions, you should review the subskills in Unit Nine for the questions you missed. If you correctly answered 16 or more of the questions in Unit Nine, you are now ready for Book Two			